Your Party

Oliver Eagleton is managing editor of *Phenomenal World* and author of *The Starmer Project: A Journey to the Right*. He is a regular contributor to the *New Statesman* and also writes for the *Guardian*, *New York Times*, *New Left Review* and *Jacobin*. He lives in London.

Your Party

The Return of the Left

*Interviews with Andrew Feinstein, Leanne Mohamad,
Andrew Murray, Alex Nunns, James
Schneider, Zarah Sultana*

Edited by Oliver Eagleton

VERSO
London • New York

First published by Verso 2025
The collection © Verso 2025
The interviews © The interviewees 2025
Introduction © Oliver Eagleton 2025

Chapters 1, 2, 3 and 5 appeared originally in
Sidecar, the blog of *New Left Review*

The manufacturer's authorized representative in the EU for product safety
(GPSR) is LOGOS EUROPE, 9 rue Nicolas Poussin, 17000, La Rochelle, France
contact@logoseurope.eu

The moral rights of the authors have been asserted

1 3 5 7 9 10 8 6 4 2

Verso
UK: 6 Meard Street, London W1F 0EG
US: 207 East 32nd Street, New York, NY 10016
versobooks.com

Verso is the imprint of New Left Books

ISBN-13: 978-1-83674-384-2
ISBN-13: 978-1-83674-386-6 (US EBK)
ISBN-13: 978-1-83674-385-9 (UK EBK)

British Library Cataloguing in Publication Data
A catalogue record for this book is available from the British Library

Library of Congress Cataloging-in-Publication Data
A catalog record for this book is available from the Library of Congress

Typeset in Sabon MT by Hewer Text UK Ltd, Edinburgh
Printed and bound by CPI Group (UK) Ltd, Croydon, CR0 4YY

Contents

Introduction

Oliver Eagleton

The character of Britain's Labour government is reflected in the killing fields of Gaza. Before his ascent to Downing Street in July 2024, Sir Keir Starmer insisted that Israel had the right to impose a siege on the Strip – cutting off power and water. Since then, he has supplied the butchers in the Israeli cabinet with the tools they need to exterminate the trapped Palestinian population. Over the course of just three months, Labour approved more arms sales than the Conservatives permitted over the previous four years. Starmer has fought tooth and nail against legal challenges to ensure that the UK can help manufacture the fighter jets Israel is using to rain hellfire down on civilian areas and 'safe zones'. Under his watch, more than 8,000 British munitions have been sent to the occupying army; hundreds of British spy planes have collected intelligence on its behalf; senior British military figures have held secret meetings with their Israeli counterparts; and British diplomats have provided cover for their atrocities. When we look at the fallout – skeletal children screaming from the pain of hunger, entire families trapped under the rubble of razed buildings, a death toll projected to reach 200,000 by the war's end – we cannot accuse Starmer of 'inaction' or 'complicity'. For he is not a bystander, but a perpetrator.

Any assessment of the current Labour Party must start with this fact, because it captures the essence of its politics: an adamantine commitment to upholding the interests of the powerful which sanctions even the most intense forms of violence, including the crime of genocide. While the effects of this outlook are most visible in Palestine, they stretch beyond those boundaries. Starmer has pounded Yemen with bombs and backed the US assault on Iran, suggesting that the UK could become directly involved in the conflict later down the line. He has embarked on a massive military build-up, with warfare spending set to reach an astonishing 5 per cent of GDP over the next decade and arms companies given access to the highest levels of government. Rather than trying to resolve the war in Ukraine, Starmer has proposed a major provocation: sending UK troops to the front line as part of a 'coalition of the willing'. Rather than calming tensions with China, his government has inflamed them by announcing that it is 'ready to fight' in the Pacific. While this spiral of jingoism may seem senseless, behind it is a consistent rationale: to reassert Britain's role as a milita-rised enclave of American empire, a nation that will spare no expense, neither in public money nor human lives, to serve Washington's objectives.

The violence of Starmerism, though, is not directed only at its external opponents. Internal enemies are similarly in the crosshairs. The government has classified Palestine Action, an organisation that disrupts arms factories assist-ing the Israeli war, as a 'terrorist' entity: consequently its supporters can be jailed for up to fourteen years. The decree is without precedent in British history. Never before has the state taken such extreme measures to eradicate a protest movement. The number of arrests to date has surpassed 1,600, with many more to follow. Elderly peace activists holding signs that read 'I oppose genocide, I support Palestine Action' are now treated as equivalent to followers of Isis or al-Qaida and manhandled into riot vans by dozens of armoured police. People involved in organising protests against the ban have been rounded up in dawn raids and charged with terrorism offences. The crackdown has been condemned by the United Nations Human Rights Chief, who described it as 'disproportionate and unnecessary'. It has also been slammed by the UK's two largest human rights organisations, Amnesty International calling it an 'egregious abuse' and Liberty warning of its 'chilling effect'.

This fits with Starmer's wider ambition to build a state that can smother any effective form of dissent. He has kept in place legislation that allows police to disband any protest they consider a 'nuisance', introduced a bill that imposes further arbitrary restrictions on demonstrations, and made it easier to deport non-citizen activists in Trumpian fashion. Branding them 'contemptible', the PM has demanded that climate campaigners be given stiffer sentences. During his time in office, environmentalists have reportedly received the harshest jail terms ever handed down to peaceful protesters in Britain: one of them getting five years for discussing a protest in an online call, another six months for participating in a 'slow march' down a London street. Laws intended to suppress organised crime rings have been creatively interpreted to apply to protest groups and lock up their members. They are backed by a major enhancement of the surveillance state, with Labour working doggedly to gain access to people's private mobile data and bringing in a 'bank spying bill' to snoop on Britons' personal accounts. A project called the National Violent Disorder Programme is meanwhile targeting perceived threats to social order by rolling out facial recognition technology across the country.

Labour's brutality abroad and repression at home are both heavily racialised, with new police powers and 'antisocial behaviour' laws often deployed against communities of colour. In the 2024 election campaign, Starmer and his shadow minister Jonathan Ashworth complained that not enough people from 'countries like Bangladesh' were being deported. Once they took the reins of government, Labour duly launched a ferocious assault on migrants: ramping up immigration raids and summarily ejecting people from the country, while broadcasting the lurid footage on social media. A new Border Security Command with a 'counterterrorism' remit has extended the militarisation of Britain's frontier – which, combined with subsidies for French authorities to wage war on the migrant population there, is supposed to prevent undesirables from reaching our shores. Starmer is currently in talks with several countries about plans to process asylum applications overseas, in a rerun of the Tories' infamous Rwanda policy. The PM has become well versed in inciting racial hatred: channelling Enoch Powell to claim that Britain has become an 'island of strangers'; accusing migrants of inflicting 'incalculable' damage on society, overstretching public services and breaching 'national security'. His administration appears to spend much of its time brainstorming innovative ways of making the lives of asylum seekers even more intolerable. Its latest scheme: to create an elaborate financial infrastructure that will ban them from buying certain 'non-essential' items, such as tickets for leisure activities and toys for their children.

Soon enough, such luxuries may be out of reach for many other working-class Britons, as Labour steps up its perma-austerity approach to the economy. While splashing out on more bombs and stronger borders, the government is also slashing vital services. One of its first acts after the election was to remove winter fuel allowances for most of the elderly, which would have forced as many as 100,000 pensioners into energy poverty were it not for a last-minute U-turn. Labour also announced that it would retain the Conservatives' two-child benefit cap, despite the policy pushing eighty children into poverty each day. Next on the chopping block was welfare, with Starmer making it his personal mission to remove support payments to sick and disabled people so as to corral them into the labour market, whether or not they are fit to work. Though public opposition has forced ministers to delay or backtrack on some of these reforms, it has not changed the overall direction of travel. A set of 'iron-clad' fiscal rules are routinely invoked by the grim-faced chancellor, Rachel Reeves, to keep spending at miserly levels and head off any demand for public investment. With the health department in a state of roiling crisis, it has been decided that its budget will increase by only 2.8 per cent annually, well below the postwar historical norm of 3.7 per cent. With local councils unable to meet their basic social obligations, the government has opted to target deprived boroughs for further cuts, sometimes exceeding 10 per cent of their budgets. As the state struggles to fulfil its essential functions, Starmer and Reeves demand even more retrenchment, with day-to-day administrative spending to fall by 16 per cent on average.

Naturally, it is private interests that stand to benefit, swooping in to fill the gaps under the auspices of 'public–private partnership'. Starmer's Labour is a champion of this model, in which profiteers become ever more embedded in the state. The former head of Amazon UK has been put in charge of regulating private monopolies. The one-time CEO of Microsoft UK now chairs the government's industrial strategy council. Lucrative contracts are being doled out to shadowy corporations, in a frame-by-frame replay of the Private Finance Initiative, while a breakneck deregulation programme has reassured such firms that they needn't consider the social fallout of their activities. Wealth thus continues to be redistributed upward to financiers and asset managers, while workers are asked to foot the tax bill and scrape by on stagnant wages.

The pattern, then, is fairly consistent. Genocide in the Middle East to protect the US–Israeli order from Palestinian resistance. Authoritarianism to defend 'British culture' from the corrupting influence of protesters and migrants. Austerity to safeguard the privileges of investors against groups like pensioners and benefits claimants. Starmerism is nothing more than the fortification of these power structures against perceived threats from outside. This is not quite the politics of New Labour, defined by faith in free markets and the cult of modernisation. It is a politics of our present: an age of anxiety, in which the establishment strives to root out agents of disruption in the interest of stability. The Labour Party today has no future orientation, no conception of 'progress'. It is a purely conservative force, seeking to preserve the decrepit institutions of the state and capital, and harking back to a time when they commanded greater confidence. This restorationist tendency is, of course, why Labour's outlook shades so easily into that of Nigel Farage's Reform UK – why the two parties share such similar rhetoric, and similar diagnoses of the country's ills. Having eradicated any trace of social democracy from Labour's ranks, Starmer now presides over an empty husk of reaction. His policies are increasingly right-populist while his communication style remains stubbornly bland-centrist. No wonder that

Farage – a more capable and combative media performer, who falsely presents himself as a force of opposition – is leading him by ten points in the polls.

Nor is it a mystery why this hard-right tendency has become so dominant in contemporary Britain. It is on the rise globally, because of the crack-up of neoliberalism and the long fallout of the Great Recession. But the most immediate local explanation can be summed up in two words: Jeremy Corbyn. His leadership of the Labour Party from 2015 to 2020 was a traumatic shock for the country's elite, as it took aim at each of the power structures mentioned above. It promised to end Britain's subservience to the US and adopt an autonomous international role; to replace its unaccountable state with a thoroughly democratised and decentralised system; and to loosen capital's stranglehold on the economy, so that the working class could take charge of it. Corbynism not only illuminated this different path for the UK; it also proved – and this was the real danger – that such a radical programme could be widely popular. Those who grew up in the shadow of the 2008 financial crisis saw possibilities in Corbyn's Labour that the traditional Westminster duopoly had tried to bury. They joined with an older generation who remembered the time before Thatcher had declared the absence of alternatives to capitalism and who had never bought this fiction. From there, the energy of Corbynism radiated to other social strata, convincing them that apathy and despair were not the only political emotions on offer, that they could be converted into anger and hope. The 2017 election confirmed this mass appeal when Corbyn won 40 per cent of the vote: more than Labour had captured in sixteen years, and the first time it had gained seats in twenty.

Immediately, the establishment mobilised to prevent a socialist government. It used a range of instruments, but by far the most lethal was the People's Vote campaign, which chipped away at Labour's position on the Brexit referendum – to respect the democratic result – and made it unelectable in crucial Leave constituencies. The most significant figure in this wrecking operation was Starmer, who became the chief Remainer in the shadow cabinet as a means of raising his profile and positioning himself as the next leader. From then on, his principal role in British politics was to eclipse the horizon of Corbynism and deflate the aspirations it had raised. He began by insisting that Britain could never become an internationalist actor outside the EU, and must instead remain bound by the free market rules of the bloc. Once the Corbyn project was felled by this position in 2019, ceding its populist energy to Boris Johnson, Starmer captured the party and set about remaking it through a comprehensive clear-out of the left. He passed new rules to make it impossible for outsider candidates to contest the leadership, stitched up the composition of local branches, and threatened MPs with suspension unless they fell in line. His principal target, however, was solidarity with Palestine, designated an 'antisemitic' thought crime that could lead to the termination of one's membership. The ensuing purge of anti-Zionists disproportionately targeted Jewish members, who were reported to be almost thirteen times more likely to be expelled than non-Jewish ones. It finally culminated in the ousting of Corbyn himself: a symbolic statement that his movement had been banished from Labour, never to return.

Now, having coasted into Number 10 thanks to low turnout and a collapse in the Tory vote, Starmer is attempting to scale up this approach to the country as a whole. The goal remains the same: to lower expectations, constrain the political imagination and narrow the scope of public discourse, so as to reconsolidate the bastions of ruling authority. But Sir Keir is a better party bureaucrat than he is a national politician, and he has – unsurprisingly – failed to secure even passive consent for this dismal programme. Labour's popularity has now fallen to 20 per cent. Its leader's approval rating is minus 41. It is challenged from the right by Farage, who, because he need not concern himself with the realities of government, can take the same ideological coordinates – racism, Atlanticism, deference to big business – and radicalise them, advocating policies that are practically unimplementable but rhetorically effective. By pushing the government's own agenda to its extreme conclusions, such as mass deportations and major tax cuts for the wealthy, Reform can contrast its strength to Labour's weakness. The latter thus finds itself forever outflanked, unable to keep pace with the tide of reaction that it has unleashed.

Yet the more interesting and authentic challenge comes from the left, whose forces have not been eradicated despite Starmer's best efforts, but have instead reestablished themselves outside the Labour Party. No longer trapped in this sinking ship, their potential is vast. It was registered most clearly by the mass movement against the Gaza genocide, which has brought millions onto the streets, opened up a gulf between public opinion and Westminster politics, caused major problems for the Anglo-Israeli weapons trade, and propelled five pro-Palestine independent candidates to Parliament. Corbyn's reelection in Islington North, beating Labour with a crushing majority, meanwhile thwarted a well-resourced campaign to banish him from public life, with the upshot that left-of-Labour politicians are now more numerous in Westminster than those on the far right. At this moment of political realignment – Labour tanking, the Conservatives moribund, Reform on the rise yet certain to undermine its anti-establishment credentials as it accrues real power – there is an urgent need to extend these gains. That can only be done by founding a new socialist party.

Corbyn has recognised this imperative and is prepared to play a leading role. Since the last election he has been involved in intense discussions with other left-wing operators and politicians about what form the project should take. There is no precedent for establishing this kind of mass democratic vehicle, and it has proven particularly difficult in the current landscape of the British left: a disparate set of campaigns, activist groups, labour organisers and community associations, plus a vanishingly small number of political figureheads, with different social bases and distinct priorities. Bringing them together in a unified organisation was always going to be fraught. From the beginning, two separate entities have been involved. One of them became known as the 'Memorandum of Understanding' (MoU) group, so named after a document drafted by the former North Tyne Mayor Jamie Driscoll; it included figures like the South African politician Andrew Feinstein and the one-time Respect Party leader Salma Yaqoob. The other was 'Collective', an organisation founded by Corbyn's former chief of staff Karie Murphy and the politician Pamela Fitzpatrick. The MoU group leant towards a federated model for the new party, while Collective has always favoured a unitary one. Corbyn insisted that the two must be brought together, despite the hesitations of some involved, so an organising committee was established for that purpose.

Zarah Sultana, the MP for Coventry South – who had been suspended from the Labour parliamentary party for repeatedly defying Starmer – joined the discussions in spring 2025. Her preference was for a unitary party, whereas Corbyn indicated that he favoured a looser federation. Yet, even so, Sultana quickly became associated with the MoU group while Corbyn remained closer to Collective. From the outset Sultana had expressed her opposition to some of Corbyn's advisers playing a prominent role in the new party, since in her view they had had a negative influence on his Labour leadership. Some of Corbyn's advisers, in turn, opposed Sultana's ambition to become co-leader, arguing that only Corbyn had the authority to lead, at least for an initial interim period. When Sultana's MoU allies brought a motion to the organising committee calling for joint leadership during the initial stages of the party's launch, they won a clear majority – but Corbyn and his allies considered the vote invalid, on the basis that Corbyn himself could not be forced to co-lead if he did not want to, and that the organising committee was not necessarily a legitimate forum in which to make this decision.

Sultana nonetheless felt that the committee had given her a mandate to announce the new party under co-leadership, so without consulting Corbyn she made a public statement on 3 July to that effect, stating that she had resigned from Labour and that 'Jeremy Corbyn and I will co-lead the founding of a new party, with other Independent MPs, campaigners and activists across the country'. In response, Corbyn confirmed that discussions were ongoing about a new party but did not mention any prospect of co-leadership. Some of his allies briefed against Sultana to the press, leading to a further deterioration in relations, and the organising committee was wound up at Corbyn's behest. It seemed as if the party might be stillborn. But the impasse was broken when one of Corbyn's ex-staffers, James Schneider, got both sides to agree to a founding conference, at which members would be empowered to make crucial decisions about the party's direction.

This plan was announced by Corbyn and Sultana on 24 July and the public were invited to register their interest in the provisionally named 'Your Party'. Its initial statement was a lucid indictment of Britain's problems – 4.5 million children living in poverty, corporations profiting off rising bills, endless wars abroad – and a set of concrete proposals to redress them: wealth taxes, public investment, nationalisation, decarbonisation and a foreign policy that values human life. The reception was astounding. More than 750,000 people signed up as supporters, dwarfing the membership numbers of every other Westminster party combined. The country's left had not been this energised since the apex of Corbynism. But the breach of trust between Corbyn and Sultana was not fully healed, and divisions reemerged over who would organise the upcoming conference.

Corbyn had put the Independent Alliance (IA) – the independent MPs who were elected in 2024, plus the more recently independent Sultana – in charge. But Sultana wanted to establish a new committee – 'gender balanced as well as racially and regionally diverse', as she put it – which would include more of her supporters. She claimed that this was the only way to ensure a democratic conference, amid fears it would be too tightly managed from the top, while Corbyn's faction insisted that such concerns were unfounded and that the IA was the only body with a truly democratic mandate to establish the party. One of the issues at stake was whether members would get to vote not only on who would lead the new outfit but also on its leadership model, allowing them to choose a co-leadership option.

The rest of the IA refused to accept Sultana's proposal for the conference committee and continued to shepherd the process itself. The polarisation between the MoU group and Corbyn's team grew more pronounced. As a result of the convoluted launch process, the former was now predominantly in control of the proto-party's finances, while the latter was primarily in charge of its data. A tentative agreement that neither group would make unilateral decisions failed to hold, allegedly because Corbyn's team sent out an email without Sultana's approval. At the same time, Schneider developed a roadmap for the founding process: invite supporters to become members, circulate draft versions of the party's core documents, organise mass regional assemblies where members can debate and amend these drafts, and finally hold the inaugural conference. This plan, made public on 15 September, was well-received by Your Party supporters. But for Sultana there was a problem: she feared that Corbyn's allies would use the membership system to strengthen their control over the party's resources, putting her in an even more marginal position. So before it could be launched, Sultana decided to open a membership portal herself without informing Corbyn. The fallout was disastrous. Corbyn and the rest of the IA issued a statement urging all Your Party supporters to ignore the 'unauthorised' email and cancel any direct debits that may have been set up. Sultana responded by claiming she had taken this action to safeguard grassroots involvement in the building of the party, describing the IA as a 'sexist boys club' and writing that 'I do not believe members will accept Karie Murphy and her associates having sole financial control of members' money and sole constitutional control over our conference'. Corbyn reported Sultana's action to the Information Commissioner's Office, rejecting the charge that she had been excluded from discussions and defending Murphy.

For a moment it was doubtful whether Your Party could survive the episode. Thankfully, though, the public demand for Corbyn and Sultana to deescalate – amplified by major figures on the international left – seemed to cut through. Both have since made conciliatory statements and insisted that the conference will go ahead. Corbyn has created a new membership system with Sultana's endorsement. The process appears to be back on-track, and lines of communication between the two teams are open, even if it will take time to repair the damage that has been inflicted on the pair's relationship and the party's reputation. The most dispiriting thing about the public row is that it was not political – Corbyn and Sultana are ideologically aligned – nor was it even procedural, since they broadly agree on how the founding process should work. It was, rather, about personalities: who should be in the driving seat, who can be trusted to respect the will of the members, who is capable of establishing the kind of party that Britain needs.

While it has wrangled over these questions, Your Party has lost sight of more salient ones. Though its general aims are obvious enough – to build a power bloc that can resist the politics of Starmer and Farage at every level, from the streets to the state, and advance a radical egalitarian alternative – there are still deep uncertainties over how the party should be constituted. Is its primary purpose to contest elections or to organise in communities, or some combination of the two? What political orientation can appeal to its social base as well as voters further afield, especially those who are trending towards Reform? Which type of democratic processes are most capable of engaging them in mass politics? How should local party branches relate to the national leadership? Should Your Party form an electoral alliance with the Greens, now under the eco-populist leadership of Zack Polanski? How will it withstand the inevitable backlash from the same forces that laid Corbynism low?

This book brings the debate around such questions, which has so far been taking place in closed meetings, into the open. Transcending factionalism and infighting, it allows key figures who have been involved in the party's formation – either as politicians, activists or advisers – to set out their positions, and places them in dialogue with one another. There are distinct visions of the proper relationship between parliamentary and popular power, the benefits of an explicitly anti-capitalist organisation or a broad progressive front, the lessons of the Corbyn years, and the project's short- and long-term priorities. These substantive issues will be far more decisive in determining the party's prospects than the individual disputes which have so far dominated the agenda. Its first conference, scheduled for November, will give members an opportunity to provide initial answers. Yet their ultimate resolution can only be the result of more sustained political discussion, organising and experimentation. As that process begins to unfold, the following interviews can serve as guide and reference point: a series of strategic prescriptions for the return of the left.

1
The Alternative

Zarah Sultana

Zarah Sultana is among Britain's most prominent socialist leaders. Born in Birmingham in 1993, she became politically active in the student movement and later in the upsurge of Corbynism: serving on the national executive of Young Labour, working as a community organiser for the party and eventually running for Parliament, where she now represents Coventry South. Her election coincided with the beginning of Keir Starmer's Labour leadership, which she has long excoriated for its reactionary outlook and petty authoritarianism. Over the past year her profile has increased significantly thanks to her trenchant opposition to the Starmer government's complicity in the Gaza genocide. Her dissent led to her suspension from the parliamentary party, and since then she has become a standard-bearer for the nascent left alternative: one of the youngest and most popular figures involved in its formation. Sultana has proposed co-leading the new party alongside Corbyn, and is part of a group working on the founding conference this autumn.

OLIVER EAGLETON: *Let's start with your political trajectory and relationship with the Labour Party. How has it evolved over time? What brought you to the decision to leave earlier this year? Do you think others on the so-called 'Labour left' will follow you?*

ZARAH SULTANA: I was formed politically by the War on Terror and the aftermath of the financial crisis. The first time I engaged with parliamentary politics was when the coalition government launched a direct attack on my generation by tripling tuition fees; I was part of the first cohort who had to pay £9,000 per year for higher education. I decided to join Labour at the age of seventeen, because at that time it seemed like there was no other party that could act as a vehicle for change. I never thought it was perfect. My local branch in the West Midlands was controlled by older men who didn't want young people – especially not young left-wing women – to be involved. When I went to study at Birmingham in 2012, the Labour clubs and societies did nothing other than host talks by right-wing MPs, so I had to find other political outlets.

In my first week of university my dad and I joined a delegation of Labour councillors and activists who went on a trip to the occupied West Bank, and it changed the way I saw myself. I had never previously thought of myself as privileged, but I realised that because of the sheer accident of where I was born and what passport I held, I was treated differently by the Israeli authorities. I watched as they harassed and abused Palestinians and then related to me as a regular human being. I went to Hebron and saw the Jewish-only roads, the communities who were coming under daily attack from settlers and soldiers. All this was hard to fathom. But it was even more confounding that we – our country, our society – were allowing this to happen. So that ignited an internationalism in me: a deep opposition to imperial power, apartheid, settler colonialism and military occupation.

Then when I got involved in the National Union of Students I realised that I wasn't the only one who felt this way. That's a really magical moment, when you discover that you're not alone in your politics. I started campaigning on issues like free education, maintenance grants, anti-racism, housing, Boycott, Divestment and Sanctions. It was only after I graduated, though, that I learned just how broken our social contract was. I really struggled to find work. I would go to the Jobcentre, look through my CV and wonder why, despite my degree and my experience, I didn't have a place in this economy. And of course I was also saddled with £50,000 worth of debt.

When Jeremy won the Labour leadership election in 2015, my immediate thought was, 'Oh my god, here is a national political operation that doesn't hate young people!' So I threw all my energy into the party's youth wing. I had already seen Jeremy speaking about the issues that were most important to me – at protests, events, picket lines – which naturally made Labour seem like somewhere I belonged. He set up a community organising unit, with the aim of developing a different type of politics rooted in people's material concerns, and I went to work for it, which allowed me to organise in my home region: areas like Halesowen, Wolverhampton and Stourbridge, all of which had voted for Brexit. We campaigned on local issues, ran trainings, identified leaders and built community power. From there I had the opportunity to run in the European elections and then in the general election of 2019, which is how I became an MP.

But today we have a very different kind of Labour Party: one that is pursuing austerity, watering down bills on workers' rights, and actively supporting genocide. I spent months push-ing the Starmer government to consider popular policies like taxes on the super-rich, nationalisation of utilities and univer-sal free school meals. I also fought against some of its worst excesses, such as keeping the two-child benefit cap, cutting winter fuel payments and disability benefits, and selling arms to the Israeli war machine. As a result, I was among the group of MPs who had the whip removed last year. When I last spoke to the party's Chief Whip, he insinuated that I was never going to be readmitted because I had criticised their complicity in Israel's war crimes. But, contrary to some false reports, they were never going to expel me from the parliamentary party; they were planning on keeping me in permanent limbo. I stood my ground. I told the Chief Whip that the genocide in Palestine was a litmus test – not just for me, but for millions of people across the country – and that it was far more important to me than my political career.

So, leaving the party has long been a matter of when, not if. But it was important for me to leave on my own terms, otherwise you give the leadership the ability to control the narrative. I chose to do so on a salient week, when the govern-ment decided to target disability benefits and to proscribe Palestine Action. There could be no clearer reflection of where Labour has ended up. Here is a party that wants to impose cuts on some of the most marginalised people in our society in order to please investors. Here is a party that, for the first time in British history, is criminalising a non-violent activist group, using the most repressive parts of the state to protect the profit margins of arms manufacturers. If these aren't red lines for you, then, frankly, you don't have any.

The Labour Party is dead. It has destroyed its principles and its popularity. Some Labour MPs who consider them-selves on the left are still clinging to its corpse. They say that by staying in they'll be able to retain their political influence. My response is simple: you haven't been able to stop disability cuts, you haven't been able to stop the flow of arms to a genocidal apartheid state, so where is this influence you're talking about? There's no point standing around waiting for a change of leadership while people are dying – not just in Gaza, but also from the poverty in this country. Time to get out, build something new, and invite everyone to join.

For many people of our generation, Corbynism set a paradigm for radical politics. Considering the historical gulf between 2015 and 2025, though, how should we adapt it to the present?

I think we're in a very different political moment. We have to build on the strengths of Corbynism – its energy, mass appeal and bold policy platform – and we also have to recognise its limitations. It capitulated to the International Holocaust Remembrance Association (IHRA) definition of antisemitism, which famously equates it with anti-Zionism, and which even its lead author Kenneth Stern has now publicly criticised. It triangulated on Brexit, which alienated huge numbers of voters. It abandoned mandatory reselection of MPs for the trigger ballot compromise, keeping many of the party's undemocratic structures in place. It didn't make a real effort to channel its mass membership into the labour movement or tenants' unions, which would have enriched the party's social base. When it came under attack from the state and the media, it should have fought back, recognising that these are our class enemies. But instead it was frightened and far too conciliatory. This was a serious mistake. If we're contesting state power, we're going to face a major backlash, and we need to have the institutional resilience to withstand it. You cannot give these people an inch.

Between 2015 and 2019 I had friends and colleagues who worked at the top of the Labour Party, and they can tell you that in parts it was a highly dysfunctional working environment with toxicity and bullying – not from Jeremy, but from some people around him. Power was too centralised. This is not what we need for this emerging project. We now have a younger generation that is highly politicised due to the establishment's disastrous policies on housing, education, employment and war. They are going to demand a seat at the table and the ability to wield actual power, and rightfully so. My vision for the new party is about that kind of active participation, because that's how I got into politics myself: not by the traditional route of running as a councillor, but through social movements. Everyone has to feel that they're involved and the organisation has to be representative of wider society. That also means we can't soft-pedal our anti-racism. Some people want us to focus solely on the 'economic issues'. But if the politics of class is detached from the politics of race then it is bound to fail – because when our neighbours are being simultaneously targeted for eviction and deportation, that struggle is one and the same.

You're right that any left project that draws an illusory dividing line between race and class will end up dividing its base, while also degenerating politically. But I also want to ask about how the party should position itself vis-a-vis Reform. Some of its messaging so far has emphasised stopping the far right and beating Farage. I think we can all agree on the necessity of that. But is there a danger that by presenting itself as primarily an anti-fascist party it could divert attention from the government as our principal adversary, or even legitimise Labour as part of some kind of popular front?

I don't think you have to choose whether to focus on Reform or Labour. You can oppose Farage and spell out what he would do to the country, and you can also attack the government for acting as Reform-lite. Remember that quote by Sivanandan, 'What Enoch Powell says today, the Conservative Party says tomorrow, and the Labour Party legislates on the day after.' Unless we challenge this Powellite politics wherever it rears its head, we're doing a disservice to the people we want to represent. It's true that we can't treat the rise of racist nationalism as simply a moral issue – we have to address its structural causes: the way it feeds off the anger and despair in areas that have been devastated by the Westminster consensus. But the right does not have a monopoly on this anger. I'm angry too. We should all be angry when we think about what's happened to these working-class communities, and we should harness those feelings to make a very clear argument – that the problem is not migrant labour but exploitative landlords, greedy energy companies, privatised services. We don't have to patronise people and tell them their frustrations are wrong, nor do we have to pander to any kind of nativism. We can be confident in our politics and communicate it through local campaigns and persuasive conversations.

This is a long process; it takes months and even years, especially in places where these arguments aren't familiar to most people. But there are ways to make them cut through. One is to talk about the kind of society we actually want, and to describe it in detail rather than just sloganeering. What are our long-term goals? More time with our loved ones, more green space, universal childcare, free public transport, not worrying about bills. These are things that Farage and Starmer don't talk about, so that allows us to contrast our positive vision with their wholly negative one.

And then there is always the question: how are we going to pay for this? Well, we can put an end to massive military overspending; we can tax the oil and gas companies; we can reverse the redistribution of wealth from the public to the private sector that has accelerated since Covid. We should pledge to fund free public transport instead of funding forever wars. These are policies that make sense to people. We need to argue for them as aggressively as the right argues for theirs.

That's a good description of the long-term horizon. What are shorter-term aims of the project?

We're still at an embryonic stage, but then again we've already got more than 700,000 people who have shown interest, so our job at this moment should be to focus on activating our base and articulating who we are – which, incidentally, is why I believe we should call ourselves 'The Left', because it's an unapologetic expression of what we stand for. At the same time we need to be recruiting from across the country, in areas that don't have the same levels of political activity that London does. We've seen a huge amount of interest in the North West and the North East, which is very exciting, and of course I'd like to see more people involved in the West Midlands. My view is that there should also be a high degree of autonomy for Scotland and Wales. A lot of unofficial local groups have also been springing up since we announced the party, but we will be formalising our structures at the upcoming conference. The overall party structure has to be unitary, otherwise it won't be a cohesive project that unites the existing spectrum of movements and struggles. A federation will not be as able to galvanise people or go on the offensive; it could end up being little more than a loose collection of different groups rather than a powerful, united bloc.

In order to establish all this we need to have a fully democratic conference. This relies on a few different things. First, it can't be led by just MPs. Right now there are six of us MPs in the Independent Alliance, five of whom are men. This shouldn't be what our party looks like going forwards, so the committee that's organising the conference should be gender balanced as well as racially and regionally diverse, all with an equal stake and voting rights. Anything less would be a boys' club. Second, those who participate in our inaugural conference have to take part meaningfully, and that can only mean 'one member, one vote'. There should be an accessible venue, as well as a hybrid aspect with low barriers to entry. We should be striving for mass participation, as opposed to a narrow delegate structure which could be unrepresentative of our base. And finally, we should have a genuine forum for debate and discussion, not a situation where decisions are made by an executive team and rubber stamped by everyone else.

All this is vital, because unless we have the right internal democratic processes from the outset it will be much more difficult for the party to act as a catalyst for any broader form of democratisation; whereas if we organise an open and pluralistic conference, we will have already broken the conventions of British politics, which is a first step on the road to reshaping them. We can then establish not only a platform that speaks to people's everyday concerns, but also a major campaigning presence across the country. We don't just want electoralism – we want a project that's tied to tenants' unions, labour organising, the fight to defend the NHS from privatisation and the Palestine solidarity movement.

To campaign effectively on all these fronts we need to make a clear set of demands. Think of Zohran Mamdani in New York; even many of us here in Britain know what his main pledges are. He has expressed them so that everyone can understand them, and they resonate on a level far deeper than most political discourse. If we start to do this then we'll realise we don't have to be beholden to the archaic traditions of Westminster, which are designed to make politics exclusionary.

Some have argued that the new party's main role should be to strengthen or create working-class institutions as a prerequisite for future electoral campaigns. Others say that the priority is to create a prominent parliamentary bloc that can make effective interventions and win elections – which, in turn, will have a spontaneously energising effect on working-class civic life. Where do you stand in this debate?

It's a false binary. I see my job in Westminster as a bridge between social movements, trade unions and Parliament. The progressive laws that we now take for granted – workers' protections, maternity leave, the weekend, even the right to vote – only came about because MPs were forced to respond to wider pressures. The struggles that forced these concessions often get erased from history. Today we see Labour MPs showing support for 'women's rights' by wearing suffragette sashes while at the same time voting to proscribe Palestine Action. We shouldn't follow their lead by acting as if there's some necessary gulf between the realms of popular and parliamentary power. A party that only cares about elections will be irrelevant outside of an election cycle. And a party that ignores Parliament will create a vacuum that will inevitably be taken up by the far right.

What I want – and I struggle to see how a successful left party could be set up in any other way – is a campaigning, social-movement orientation combined with a robust parliamentary presence: a situation where our MPs are on the front lines of strike actions and anti-fascist mobilisations. If you focus entirely on Parliament rather than building wider capacity, that's a very short-termist approach, because what happens when those MPs are attacked by the establishment? What happens if they lose their seats or they retire? You need to build the social infrastructure that will support them in office and identify new leaders to replace them. It's that kind of community power that sustains socialist politicians and holds them to account. Without that, you either get capitulation, or you get a left that's dominated by a few figureheads at the top, which makes it formally indistinguishable from every other party.

The thing is, people recognise when politicians are inauthentic, when they have no connection to a popular base. They see through it immediately. Whereas when you're the kind of politician like Jeremy Corbyn or John McDonnell or Diane Abbott, whose authority is deeply rooted in community struggles, you have a very distinct profile, and you can make much more meaningful gains.

When it comes to certain strategic decisions, however, there might be some binary choices. For example, should the party set up its own community organising unit (COU), like the one you used to work for, or should it leave community organising to the communities?

In theory, I love the idea of having mass community organising as part of the DNA of the party. There are people who are already doing the everyday work of making sure that no one in their community goes hungry, or that the far right cannot attack asylum hotels. The new party should be finding those people – who don't necessarily fit the traditional notions of a political leader – and getting them involved, asking them to shape the organisation, cultivating them for positions of authority. But should this take the form of a community organising unit such as we had in the Labour Party? Here I think there are certain limitations. In my experience, the COU didn't always get the victories that it deserved, partly because when this kind of community work is attached to a party it immediately comes with certain connotations, which might be off-putting to those who are understandably fed up with party politics. We also had situations where the COU came into conflict with other parts of the Labour Party, for example, when councils weren't paying their workers a fair wage. I'm not saying this would happen with the new project, but there's always the danger that when a national party is doing a range of different organising activities they may not fit together perfectly and tensions may arise.

Community organising would be more effective if, rather than being run by a specific unit, it becomes an ingrained practice across the party – in how we run meetings, training sessions, canvassing and campaigns. The role of the party could be to develop this kind of mass political culture: to make it second nature for people to engage in politics at ground level, so that they would go and set up tenants' unions, book clubs, anti-raids groups, or whatever else would meet their local needs. That way, the party would play a role in stimulating popular struggles without having to manage and control them. Political education would be a vital part of that: translating people's instinctive sense of what's wrong with society into a radical outlook. If we got half the people who've signed up as supporters into political education, the effects would be transformative. It's impossible to predict where that would lead.

That's interesting. So, the party wouldn't necessarily be tasked with forming these institutions, but nor would it assume that they will just spring up spontaneously. It would instead use its local democratic structures and education initiatives to create the political culture that would spur people to get active. One thing that's certain to militate against all this is needless factionalism. What of the divisions that have beset the project so far?

After I announced my resignation and intention to co-lead the founding of a new left party with Jeremy, the leaks against me were almost instantaneous. A small number of people who are involved in the party have engaged in anonymous briefings, making hostile and implicitly Islamophobic comments about me to the *Sunday Times* and *Sky News*. This behaviour is absolutely unacceptable in any context, but especially one in which we're trying to create a new political culture. People who are supposedly on the left thinking it's appropriate to use the Murdoch press to broadcast smears is astounding. This is the very same media class who tried to destroy Jeremy's reputation and the politics he represents. There is no space for that in what we're building. We all understand comradely disagreement, but it's different when you cross class lines for the sake of factionalism and psychodrama. The members don't want that; it's a major turn-off for them. I personally have no time for this type of bullying and intimidation, and I'm not going to let it sabotage a project that's much bigger than all of us. We have fascism growling at the door; egos have no place in this fight.

A devil's advocate argument against a fully member-led party model might go something like the following. Because we don't yet have a mass political culture, many people who want to be politically active don't know quite what that would entail. They might therefore want to have their energies directed, rather than doing all the directing themselves. The absence of mass politics also means that the organised left consists of various relatively small groups with their own distinct priorities, which will be difficult to bring together in a unified structure without intervention from above. And there is also the related risk that some of these priorities might not be particularly representative of society at large. What would you say to this?

If we follow that argument, we'll just replicate the problems with every single other political party: top-down control, unaccountable decision-making, internal bickering, jobs handed out to mates. I find the case against member-led democracy bizarre given that our entire aim is to empower people. You simply cannot do this without getting people involved and giving them ownership over the policies, strategy and leadership. This will inevitably result in some difficult situations, with various positions and perspectives coming up against one another, but that's to be expected. If there are certain issues where we can't convince a majority, then we can't just circumvent or ignore them; that would be an abdication of political responsibility. Instead, we have to work harder. I have no qualms, for instance, about advocating a resolutely anti-racist and pro-trans socialist programme, even if parts of that sounds contentious to some people. It's only by having these discussions out in the open and through the proper channels that we can create something that looks fundamentally different, feels fundamentally different, to the other Westminster parties. If that's not the aim, what are we doing here?

While we're on the subject of the other parties, what is your view on electoral alliances?

I'm open to electoral alliances, with the caveat that this would have to be supported by the members. In general, I think we should be willing to work with anyone who will help us beat the right and the establishment. We need to be pragmatic, especially as long as we're working within the first-past-the-post system, although winning electoral reform should be an objective as well. But at this point it would be premature to start carving up the constituencies – deciding where we should run, where we might stand aside – when we haven't yet understood the full extent of what we're building. Until we've actually created the party, and gotten a sense of its capabilities and its limits, we can't do that in any detail. It's going to be four years until the next general election. We first have to develop the party's structures, and then the negotiations about that kind of strategy will come later if the members approve them.

What are the benefits of a co-leadership model, with you and Corbyn at the helm?

If we have more voices at the top, if we avoid concentrating power in one pair of hands, then we will be more representative of our movement and more accountable to it. It's no small thing to start a new party; there's a lot to be done and we need to share the work. So it seems natural that two people with the same values and principles, and the same belief in the project, should do it together. We have a lot to learn from each other; I'm always learning from Jeremy and I'd like to think there are insights I can offer him as well. A co-leadership with equal powers would mean that neither of us is a tokenistic figure. It would also allow us to take what is often just a liberal soundbite about 'more women in leadership roles' and make it a reality, undermining the prejudices that usually hold young women back: not serious enough, too inexperienced and so on. People are already hugely excited about this idea and they've been getting in touch in vast numbers. It's not about shying away from strong leadership, but about doubling its strength.

What can supporters do ahead of the conference? How can they be most useful?

Mass recruitment is crucial. We will need to organise events in the run-up to the conference to enthuse supporters and recruit more people. One of the best parts of Corbynism was the rallies and the music and the performances. We need to get that back. What we need is a politics of fun and joy. We're not interested in meetings where everyone's got a point of order and they talk for twenty minutes each. Do you think the sixteen-year-olds who are soon to get the vote will want to sit through that? The new project should engage that generation by embedding itself in mass culture. We've already seen musicians, artists, actors lining up to get involved. Jade Thirlwall has been supportive, so has Aimee Lou Wood and Ambika Mod – people in that younger age bracket who are in touch with popular sentiment and who know how far removed it is from the decaying politics of the establishment. We must do politics differently and that's not a cliché, but a prerequisite for this party.

The goal is to change politics forever. When we have a government abetting genocide and waging war on its own citizens, and a far right gearing up to enter Downing Street, we can't deny the urgency. So, I am ready to give everything to this fight. That's what I owe to my community and to my class. Now's the moment.

2
Building the Party
James Schneider

One of the key organisers working on the new party is James Schneider. Born in 1987, Schneider was radicalised by the war on Iraq and the global financial crisis. He co-founded the campaign group Momentum to build popular support for Corbyn's leadership in 2015 and was recruited as the party's director of strategic communications a year later: a role in which he advocated an unapologetic form of left-populism, trying – ultimately in vain – to resist pressure to capitulate to the Labour right on key issues such as Brexit. Since then he has published Our Bloc *(2022), his blueprint for the future of the British left, and he now works as communications director for the Progressive International.*

OLIVER EAGLETON: *Let's start with your general account of what a left party should hope to achieve in the political landscape of the 2020s – especially in a country like Britain, where it would face a number of major obstacles, from the grip of the establishment media to the antidemocratic Westminster system to the division of left-of-Labour forces.*

JAMES SCHNEIDER: The task of this party should be to undertake different forms of 'political construction'. First there is the construction of popular unity: taking the constituencies that currently form a sociological majority and translating them into a political majority. In Britain these are the asset-poor working class, downwardly mobile graduates and racialised communities. Most people think about constituencies in purely electoral terms: 'How can we win a few more seats?' and so on. But it doesn't fundamentally matter whether you have fifty or a hundred or two hundred MPs unless your electoral strategy is linked to this wider social project.

Then there is the construction of popular power: building structured organisations that people can use to democratically control different parts of their lives, either by winning concessions from capital and the state, or by partially transcending them – decommodifying certain resources or carving out autonomous spaces. This allows people to collectively legislate from below while at the same time creating the conditions for their party to legislate from above. Britain's labour movement and cooperatives have traditionally served this purpose. Other countries have more varied traditions of creating popular power, through tenants' groups, agricultural collectives, debtors' unions and land occupations, to name just a few.

That brings us to the final form of political construction: that of a popular alternative. Popular unity and popular power demonstrate that there are alternative ways to organise society as a whole, while also building a majoritarian programme for government that is capable of meeting people's needs in the short to medium term. If we pursue this tripartite strategy, then we will begin to see the emergence of new forms of popular protagonism that diffuse struggle and control throughout society.

Let me give you two examples from Colombia. This was historically one of the continent's main outposts of imperialism, dominated by a conservative comprador elite. Yet for more than seventy years, the country's oil has been publicly owned, because oil workers launched an indefinite strike in 1948 that forced the state to establish a nationalised company, and persistent mass pressure means that no government since has been able to reverse the decision. More recently, in 2010, an institution called the People's Congress was formed to bring together various social movements and territorial struggles: urban, peasant, indigenous. One of their initiatives was to set up peasant-controlled food-producing territories that linked small farmers with the urban poor, and they eventually forced the government to recognise and support these expanding territories – which are conceived by the movement as 'trenches of popular power'. This strategy of legislating from below fed into the election of Colombia's first-ever left-wing government in 2022, led by Gustavo Petro.

To summarise, our party needs to be a vehicle for establishing unity, a catalyst for popular organising and a lever for popular mobilisation towards a social alternative. Our long-term aim, far beyond what can be achieved in the 2020s, should be to establish a society that recognises the essential dignity of every person. While this principle is self-evident to many, the macrostructures of our global system stand firmly against it. The current order is built on a triad of capital, the nation and the state. Our aim should be to replace it with a different one: the social, the international and the democratic – three interlocking logics that open space for new forms of life beyond exploitation, empire and top-down control. That means socialising the economy, transforming our position in the chain of imperial relations and the global division of labour, and democratising the state. There is no path to a sustainable ecological future without these transformations. In this country, we've never had a vehicle that has tried to effect this kind of change through mass politics. None of the small left groups has done so. Even under Corbyn's leadership of the Labour Party, we did not conceive of our goal in these terms. What it requires is a people's party, and a surrounding set of organisations, which can win power in every sense: social, cultural, political, industrial.

Can you say more about how this strategy would grapple with the practical realities of British politics today?

The social constituencies I outlined above – asset-poor workers, downwardly mobile graduates and racialised people – would benefit most from a movement to abolish the present state of things. Of course, a left party should also seek to win support beyond these groups: there are progressive elements outside them just as there are reactionary elements within them, so it can't be a rigid or mechanical process. But these are the three main actors through which popular unity can be forged. Some of the reasons why they make up a numerical majority are related to Britain's global position as an advanced economy in the capitalist core, but others are more specific: for example, the policies pushed through by New Labour in higher education, housing and industry, which created the category of the downwardly mobile graduate (ironically, since New Labour was in part the project of an upwardly mobile graduate class). Increasingly, the actions of the establishment – especially the present Labour government – are consolidating a common interest among these constituencies. The Westminster parties have immiserated the asset-poor along with younger graduates, and they have tried to place the blame on racialised people, including those who do not fit within these other two social categories, which gives them a shared basis for overturning the status quo.

So, the potential is there. What's lacking is the capacity. When it comes to popular power, we are starting from a very low level. Civic life in Britain, as in much of the Global North, has been rubbed to a residue. Working-class associational life has been smashed; not just the unions and cooperatives, but the libraries, the pubs, the clubs, the bands, the sports teams. Fewer and fewer people even remember this earlier political culture. Our strongest manifestation of popular power is the labour movement, and the main thing it has experienced over the last fifty years is defeat, which naturally creates a defensive posture. How do we overcome it? Well, popular power is always based on density. There's a reason why the factory creates political openings for the left – and the same goes for the working-class neighbourhood – as a site where people naturally come together. In Britain this has clear implications for electoral strategy because of the first-past-the-post system. I am no apologist for that system, but it happens to exist and we must work within it for the time being. One thing it forces us to do is pursue a strategy of density: rooting our project in specific areas in which those three social constituencies have a supermajority.

Let's look at the election last year, where the five independents running to the left of Labour won seats in Parliament: a relatively small gain, but also a historic one, in that there had previously been only three left-of-Labour independents since the Second World War. The situation in Islington North, where Corbyn beat the Labour challenger by a crushing margin, was somewhat *sui generis* in that he was a candidate with a national profile and 100 per cent name recognition. It has wider implications, however, in that every last remaining element of social power was mobilised in support of the campaign, precisely because people saw it as an expression of *their own* civic life. Every gardening group, every church, every mosque, every trade union branch in the area – they all recognised that Corbyn was their political embodiment, which is why they turned out for him, almost regardless of what they thought about specific policies.

The four other independents also won largely on account of the real social power in their communities, which is largely based in the mosques – although, of course, many non-Muslims and non-practising Muslims campaigned and voted for them as well. People go to mosque every week. It's a place of sociality, a place of welfare, a place of moral direction. And so, even though these independent candidates would be the first to admit that they were politically inexperienced – that they didn't have slick campaigns or cutting-edge communications or a comprehensive policy platform – they were nonetheless carried to victory through this identification with the community's power centre, which helped to channel their shared revulsion at the genocide in Gaza along with a range of other issues. That's exactly why the establishment reacted with such horror. It was not just a matter of Islamophobia; it was also a terrified recognition that popular power can bypass the structures that are supposed to neutralise it.

If your ambition is to create some kind of binding link between a political party and wider forms of associational life, then perhaps there is a distinction to be drawn between movements and institutions. The first can be ephemeral and amorphous, failing to create durable forms of popular power, in the absence of the second. You might say that, when it comes to issues like the Gaza genocide, it is the movement which activates people as political subjects, the institution which translates that politicisation into popular power, and the party which harnesses that power to influence or capture the state. Which leads me to ask: if Britain's working-class institutional culture has been largely destroyed over the past half-century, leaving behind only isolated enclaves, then aren't we missing a crucial link in this sequence? How should a new left party address this problem?

We need to construct more institutions. This, for me, is the most important strategic task for the party and also the one that is most likely to be overlooked. As well as strengthening the manifestations of popular power that have survived in the ruins of neoliberalism, we must create new ones. The number of rented households in the UK is 8.6 million. The number of people in tenants' unions is roughly 20,000. Only 38 per cent of tenants voted in the last election. If, under Corbyn's Labour, we had decided to go out and knock on doors and organise tenants, how many tenant leaders would we now have? How could we have shifted the consciousness of the Labour left, away from cheerleading for a parliamentary party on Twitter and towards building strong institutions of its own? You could ask the same questions about a range of other issues. With 600,000 Labour members, 450,000 of whom were on the left, we could have decided that it was a political priority to organise around issue X or Y. If we had mobilised even 10 per cent of those left-wing members we could have set up new popular organisations: food cooperatives, bill payers' unions, mental health groups. You could have had campaigns building for a climate strike or trying to bring utilities into public ownership through mass boycotts. There's no shortage of possibilities, and it's not my place to be prescriptive about which of them we should prioritise over the coming years. These choices need to be made democratically by a national political party.

If the new party spends all its time working out the perfect social care policy for our imaginary left-technocratic future when we run the state, it will go nowhere. If it views itself as a Labour Party 2.0, with better politics than the current one but with no outlets for real popular participation, it will be destroyed by countervailing powers. During the Corbyn period we were trapped in a position where Labour members were often stuck waiting for a handful of people at the top to make decisions rather than becoming agents and leaders themselves. We cannot repeat that mistake. I think it's important to remember that outside of Europe and North America, political meetings don't suck. They aren't boring. They're lively, participatory and rooted in popular culture – with music, food, even dancing. Normal people show up because they belong. There are different ways for people to participate. And that's because their purpose is to strengthen the bonds of solidarity and unity so that people can go out and engage in the construction of popular power.

How should the new party you're envisioning go about creating this kind of non-traditional-British political culture?

In contemporary Britain, the establishment has no story to tell: it says that everything is basically fine, and you should shut up about your problems. The reactionary bloc, meanwhile, says that everything is bad: you can't get an NHS appointment, housing is unaffordable, your pay has gone down, and the reason for all this is Muslims, migrants and minorities. When these are the only two narratives on offer, then the latter is likely to win, because at least it speaks to some real grievances. But the truth is that attacking minorities is itself a minority position. There might be a certain type of pervasive racism in Britain, but most people really do not spend their time thinking about how much they hate foreigners, so there is a clear opening for a different narrative. What we should be offering instead is 'class war with a grin'. We should reject all the pieties of the political-media-state class, for they are hated by the public, and rightly so. We should create controversies rather than retreating from them.

This communicative style is often called left-populism. It involves drawing a big, bold line of antagonism in which there is unity on our side and division on the other. That line of antagonism is extremely simple: the reason for our problems is the bankers and the billionaires. They are at war with us, so we are going to war with them. We should aim to baffle and outrage the media establishment with a political style that is combative but also joyful. We should have meetings like those I've been describing, with music and food and discussion groups, and where people can come away with clear actions to carry out. This naturally means that the party should be based mostly outside Westminster; it should not be associated with blokes in suits who spend their time mumbling disingenuously to news cameras.

My dream is a party that hits with the same impact as 'Turn the Page', the opening track on The Streets' debut album *Original Pirate Material*. Something you've never heard before, yet instantly recognisable; unmistakably British and rooted in everyday life, from the pubs to the pavements. A sound – or in our case, a politics – that effortlessly blends cultures and traditions, anchored in class and community but moving forwards with confidence and style. We need to inhabit this sort of national-popular register. To put it in a more theoretical way, the efficacy of this kind of politics stems from unlocking the potential progressive valence of the 'national' dimension of the capital-nation-state triad.

You mentioned Colombia as a model, but let's think for a moment about the historical and contextual differences. There, you had a state dominated by the two main parties, the Liberals and Conservatives, who spent decades collaborating with the US to keep the country in a condition of peripheral dependency while excluding the popular sectors from power. Many of those sectors were therefore largely unintegrated into the processes of economic accumulation and political participation, which helped to forge certain autonomous traditions of struggle: guerrilla movements that controlled large parts of the countryside, campaigns against extractivism, groups defending indigenous territories. Petro was able to unify many of these forces in his electoral project, bringing the outsiders – the 'nobodies', as they were affectionately called – into the heart of government. In Britain, by contrast, the long-running problem has been less one of popular exclusion than popular assimilation. The Labour Party has traditionally been a tool to subsume the working class into the state and reconcile it with imperialism, with the upshot that our culture of popular struggle is less active; our left-wing meetings are more boring; the organic basis for this kind of mass politics is much weaker.

The Corbyn leadership had a sober assessment of these conditions. Your aim was not necessarily to empower 'the grassroots' and hope they would carry you to victory. It was, rather, to exploit a situation of political crisis, capture state power, and implement a programme of non-reformist reforms that would in turn galvanise broader swathes of people, by strengthening workers, renters, migrants and so on. This approach, in which politics from above precedes politics from below, was not simply a strategic blunder. It was a reflection of our particular historical situation and the political possibilities it generated. One could argue that those same conditions have also shaped the way in which the plan for a new left party has so far been developed, with decisions being made by a relatively small stratum of political operators who hope – not unreasonably – to use electoral victories to stimulate wider struggles.

The explanation you lay out is broadly correct and helps to account for why the predominant consciousness on the British left is highly electoralist. I'm not arguing against winning elections or going into government. I think that is essential. But there are two reasons why it can and must be combined with these other processes of political construction from the outset. First, the assimilation of the British working class – not just via the Labour Party but also the unions during the corporatist period – was never total: there were always popular revolts and sites of resistance. So, there are radical traditions on which to build. Second, we are now approaching the end of a decades-long capitalist offensive that aimed to destroy such resistance. This was done partly through assimilation but mainly through brute force: the violent exclusion of the masses in both the Global North and the Global South, with British miners getting their heads smashed in and Argentine leftists being thrown from helicopters. What we are seeing today is this onslaught beginning to stall, not because of external opposition but because of its own internal limitations: the inability of the US to hold down Chinese sovereign development, especially after 2008; and the increasing strain on resources as the ecological crisis gathers pace. This creates a vital opportunity for a left party.

But we cannot simply replay Corbynism in this context. We are not at the head of a party of government and we have no chance of getting there any time soon. So that particular electoralist-only wager, which was defeated in the first place, is even less feasible now. The number of people who were even conscious of the 2015–19 strategy as you describe it was also extremely limited: only a handful among the shadow cabinet and senior advisors who would have articulated it in that way. The logic of parliamentary socialism remained very much intact. I think we need a fundamental shift in our strategic vision in order to create a consensus on the left that recognises the importance of popular power.

If you want a negative example, then you can look at the Green Party. Its approach is to elect its candidates to public office so that they can use their profile to advocate for progressive policies. On their own terms they have had some success, electing an MP during the 2019 to 2024 period and four since then, plus many local councillors. But what impact have they had on public consciousness? Virtually none. Extinction Rebellion and Fridays for the Future have had a much more tangible effect on mass environmental politics. The Greens' mathematical approach – the more elected representatives the better – is two hundred years old, dating to the time of the liberal revolutions, when public discourse took place in newly formed parliaments and assemblies in which the numbers really mattered. It is totally unsuited to the 2020s. The party's most vocal spokesperson isn't even an MP. We've recently been hearing things like 'Together with the Greens, a left party could hold the balance of power in Westminster'. This is the same kind of self-deluding nonsense that some in the Socialist Campaign Group have been peddling for years: 'If we just stay in Labour and keep our heads down, maybe we'll hold the balance of power.' How has that worked out?

It's a liberal popular-front model that implicitly commits the left to propping up a Labour government, which would be moral and political suicide. But to stick for a moment with the lessons from Corbynism: most people recognised that one of the main reasons for its defeat was its lack of a strong social base, which made it more difficult to fight back against the smear campaigns and political sabotage to which the project was subjected. But after 2019 many of those people set about 'building the base' in a way that was detached from any larger national infrastructure, giving rise to a set of disparate initiatives – a community union here, a direct-action group there – which the government of the day has mostly ignored or repressed.

It's now widely accepted that a synthesis of electoral and popular organising is needed, as you say, but there is still no consensus on what form that should take. There's been a lot of debate over whether this new organisation should be a party from the outset or whether it should start off as an electoral alliance. Advocates of the latter would argue that the fragmented situation of the British left, and of British civic life as a whole, means that we need a coalitional structure that can encompass local struggles and support community leaders who may not explicitly identify with 'the left', even if they broadly share our politics. Yet, at the same time, a loose coalition threatens to institutionalise the left's fractured situation rather than repair it. Where do you stand on such questions?

I'm not in favour of either position, at least not their extreme versions. On the one hand, you risk having a reheated

Labourism with better politics but a similar party form, whose first priority is to find candidates to run in local elections. On the other, the danger is that we end up with a loosey-goosey umbrella of independents that offers no governmental perspective for real change. Neither of these is going to build genuine power in society.

In the book I wrote after the 2019 defeat I argued for a federation of the existing movements, structured organisations and forces on the left that could act as a building block for a more ambitious project. Today, it's still perfectly plausible that a federated organisation could play this role: laying the foundations for these different kinds of political construction I discussed earlier. But, for one thing, you would still need a unified decision-making structure to be able to set up any kind of larger structure, whether it's federal, confederal or central. Opting for a coalition over a party would not change the fact that people first need to come together and agree on the basic contours, and so far this has failed to happen. Nor is there any reason why a party can't respect diverse positions, with different tendencies and internal pluralism. An existing local political brand should be able to continue operating with a high level of autonomy, if it is so wished. These are frankly second-order issues that can be worked out when we've established the proper deliberative channels.

My preferred model would be a structure where we entrust strategy to the membership and tactics to the leadership layer. Major strategic questions – which type of social-power building to prioritise, how to distribute resources to activists across the country, what kind of political education and training to provide, what the content of the political programme should be: all this would be decided collectively. Tactics, meaning how these strategic goals are delivered, can then be determined largely by frontline organisers or politicians. In order for this to work, there would have to be a collective leadership system. It could go something like the following. A leadership slate of twelve or fifteen would run on a strategy proposal and perhaps also political proposal which it would submit to the members, who would cast single-transferrable votes for their preferred strategy and associated candidates. That would produce a national committee composed of leaders from different slates, who would then synthesise the various proposals and put them to the members' conference, where they could be approved or amended or rejected. The committee would also elect people to different national roles: our lead spokesperson, our lead organiser, our liaison with progressive movements, our party manager and so on. That way you would still have people in identifiable leadership positions, but it wouldn't just be a popularity contest. It would create a stratum of leaders who are able to make agile, tactical decisions, but it would also cultivate popular protagonism by turning strategy into a collective endeavour.

Had a left vehicle launched sooner, it could have seized a number of political opportunities. At elite level it could have exploited Starmer's decision last July to suspend seven MPs, including Sultana, from the parliamentary party, perhaps convincing more of them to jump ship. At mass level it could have mounted a united left response to the rising tide of racist violence incited by both Starmer and Farage. Why in your view has the project taken this long to come into public view?

I've been working on this for about a year now, and I think there are structural factors which make it difficult to launch anything: not just the specific type of left party I've been advocating, but any type of left party. As I've already said, it comes down to the issue of decision-making. What decisions are legitimate? Who can take them and who can implement them? There's a chicken-and-egg dilemma in which you can't make decisions until you have a structure, but to have a structure you need to make decisions. In other equivalent situations, this problem is circumvented in one of three ways.

The first is the intervention of a hyperleader. Jean-Luc Mélenchon says, 'The Parti de Gauche isn't working, I'm forming La France Insoumise,' and that's what happens. People follow him. In Britain we don't have that type of figure. We have a kind of hyperleader in Jeremy, a person whose moral and political authority towers above anyone else's; but he doesn't act in that way. It's not his style.

The second is a preexisting structured organisation with disciplined decision-making capacity. That could be a trade union or a political campaign. In South Africa, Abahlali baseMjondolo, a movement of people who live in informal shack dwellings, has 180,000 members across 102 housing settlements and is carrying out land occupations in four provinces. I went to their general assembly when I was observing the elections in South Africa last year and witnessed their discussions about building their own electoral vehicle. They can use their existing democratic mechanisms which allow decisions to be made, challenged and overturned as part of an open process where everyone knows where they stand. That, too, is missing in Britain.

The third solution is a small group of closely aligned, politically advanced people who can make decisions collectively. There have been many communist parties throughout history which have been formed by twelve or so individuals sitting around a table, which in short order became mass vehicles. But here the discussions are taking place among people with very different backgrounds and priorities who lack this collective outlook.

As a result of these three structural factors you have a further contingent factor that looms very large. It is, in fact, the determining factor, even though it is downstream from the others. That is the issue of personalities. At moments of collective inadequacy such as this one, individual problems come to the fore. This becomes much more decisive in conditions of objective paralysis. But now, thankfully, it looks like progress is being made. A new party is taking shape despite these obstacles, because both the political need and the external pressure for it are overwhelming. You cannot not build a new party when your as-yet-unnamed party is already tied with the governing party in the polls. It is going to happen in some form.

What are the plans for the official launch?

Unfortunately, the party has already been launched even though it does not exist. We have been deprived of a carefully planned launch, but we can live with that. What we need to do now is to minimise the importance of the contingent human factor by creating a different kind of sovereign authority: a body that has the power to drive the process forwards. What that looks like in practice is this democratic conference. It can be responsible for setting up a committee that would then have real legitimacy in its decision-making. Every person who signs up as a member of the party should have the full right to participate. The conference must bring them all together, with hybrid facilities and fully online voting. It could elect a collective leadership team that would be trusted to develop the organisation over the next year or so, and we could then develop structures and cultures that will allow for more meaningful decisions to be made. None of this would be perfect. In fact it would be very suboptimal, as it basically means building the car while driving. All kinds of mistakes could be made which may have ramifications further down the line. But it would at least accelerate the process. It would offer some hope at a political moment when it is in desperately short supply. And that would be a very significant thing.

3
Force of Opposition
Andrew Murray

Andrew Murray is a writer, trade unionist and political strategist. Born in 1958, he joined the Morning Star *as a lobby journalist at the age of nineteen. He moved sidelong into the labour movement in the 1980s, playing a key role in the foundation of Unite, one of the country's largest unions, and later serving as its chief of staff. During the 2000s he was appointed to the executive committee of the Communist Party of Britain and co-founded the Stop the War Coalition, set up to oppose the invasions of Iraq and Afghanistan. An early supporter of Corbyn's leadership, Murray was seconded from Unite to assist with its 2017 general election campaign before joining the team as a special political adviser. He is also the author of numerous books on UK politics: a devastating indictment of railway privatisation,* Off the Rails *(2002); an account of the structural processes that produced the Corbyn project,* The Fall and Rise of the British Left *(2019); and an analysis of the political lessons to be drawn from that experience,* Is Socialism Possible in Britain? *(2022).*

OLIVER EAGLETON: *Why, in your view, is there a political opening for this new party? What is it about the state of contemporary Britain that gives it a chance of success?*

ANDREW MURRAY: You could say that the current political opening was created by the 2008 crash. Since then, the ruling establishment has been unable to maintain the neoliberal economic model in a way that satisfies people's aspirations and has also been unwilling to replace it with a different framework. This means that British politics has been more or less running on empty. Corbyn's leadership of the Labour Party expanded the Overton window of what was ideologically acceptable, shifting it away from the very narrow parameters of Thatcherism and Blairism, and making the idea of radical social democracy – which had been completely marginalised since the end of the postwar period in the 1970s – mainstream again. This was reinforced by the mass movements against war and austerity, which generated a huge amount of political energy.

From 2020 onward there was a concerted attempt by Starmer's Labour Party to shut this opening. But he did not try to close it down by winning the argument. Instead he relied simply on coercion: suspending MPs, driving Corbyn out of the party, denying local branches the right to choose their candidates, and later taking the same authoritarian approach to society at large, with the extraordinarily repressive clampdown on Palestine solidarity. As we can see from the response to the new party's announcement – with well over half a million people already signed up as supporters – Starmer's strategy has failed. The forces mobilised by the Corbyn leadership, and turbocharged by the movement around Gaza, are still present, still active, and seeking some form of political expression, in a context where both Labour and the Tories have refused to address the underlying problems that flowed from the global financial crisis.

How can the party provide that kind of political expression?

Well, that is the main question. Debates about the organisation's structure (federal, coalitional, central) or even its leadership (sole, joint, collective) are secondary to its political positioning. The new party needs to be absolutely, clearly anti-capitalist and anti-imperialist. It needs to see itself as creating the space for a transition to socialism. Parts of its political profile can perhaps be assumed: certainly its position on Gaza and its opposition to austerity. But it needs to go further, in my view, by generalising outward from these two urgent issues and offering a systemic alternative.

This is, broadly speaking, what the party's supporters want. It is also what millions of people across the country are craving, including many of those who are gravitating towards Reform. In the present political landscape you have a crumbling centrism identified with Starmer and with Rishi Sunak before him, which takes a managerial approach to the colossal problems that have accumulated since 2008, and then you have a right-wing pseudo-opposition which the *FT*'s Martin Wolf rightly describes as 'plutocratic populism', which engages in all sorts of demagoguery, including posing as pro-worker, when in fact it is the project of millionaire Thatcherites. With this as the current polarisation, the left has a unique opportunity to redraw the lines of division: placing the centre and the hard right on one side, and itself on the other. The issues that it can use to do so are clear: opposition to austerity, opposition to medieval levels of social inequality, and opposition to war. Our slogan in the

Stop the War Coalition is 'Welfare not Warfare'. The government's might as well be 'Make the Poor Pay for War'. It is right now embarking on a major military build-up while slashing social spending – and it is doing so in lockstep with the pluto-populists, who don't even pretend to have the same non-interventionist inclinations as Trump's national-populists in the US.

So, undoubtedly, there is a political space to be occupied. Corbyn's leadership filled it from 2015 to 2019, but it was tethered to the Labour Party, which already had an entrenched position in the British status quo that many of its parliamentarians and staffers were determined to defend. The new party is in a very different situation. It will be unencumbered by these problems; it will be a novel and galvanising force. But at the same time it will not have the strength that comes from being a part of the political fabric for 120 years, nor the historical roots and power bases which, although they have massively atrophied for the Labour Party, have not disappeared entirely.

Let's talk more about what it would mean for the party to articulate a systemic alternative, especially when it comes to the UK economy. The Corbyn leadership tried to draw distinctions between productive and predatory capital, hoping to empower the first at the expense of the second: pitting green industry against big finance and so on. But in some respects this was more of a radical extension of Ed Miliband's lukewarm domestic platform than it was a resolutely socialist programme. It had a structural critique of British capitalism – emphasising the outsized power of the City – but it also reflected the extraordinary political pressure your team was under at the time: to capitulate, to accommodate, to soften your stance. Given that the new party won't face the same kind of pressure from within its ranks, do you think it will find it easier to take bolder positions than Corbynism 1.0?

Breaking the power of capital is going to be a huge challenge, to state the obvious. My view was that, had Corbyn got into power, we should have advanced our agenda on the basis of our democratic mandate and then dealt with obstructions as they arose, whether from the House of Lords or the City of London or the security services or Washington. John McDonnell was very strong as shadow chancellor; I have almost nothing but praise for how he played his role there. But I didn't agree with him when he said that Labour would not implement capital controls, because that locks you into the Starmer–Reeves position of operating within the coordinates set by the markets. By not forswearing capital controls you immediately adopt a much more confrontational approach to capital, and you are forced to think through how you would respond to its resistance. The fact is that any movement towards socialism in this country is going to have to involve a period of relative autarky and disengagement from the world-system. During this period, the aim should be to encourage people to seize control of their own political and economic destinies – taking advantage of the very low esteem in which parliamentarism is already held.

You're right that the new party has an opportunity to forge this kind of agenda without being subject to internal sabotage. From the beginning, Corbyn faced intense opposition from the majority of MPs, the party apparatus, and a whole host of established structures and procedures that shaped his leadership, as well as the external forces seeking to undermine him. Yet one of the decisive factors that led to the unravelling of the project, quite possibly the single most decisive one, was its position on Brexit. Here, the entirely incoherent and inane policy Labour ended up with in 2019 was driven in part by the establishment, but also by the party membership. Six years later, Brexit is not going to be a problem for the new party; no one is campaigning for its reversal. But similar internal tensions could still resurface on other questions, and we have to be mindful of how we manage them. It might seem like we're getting ahead of ourselves in discussing how to take power when, as yet, this entity has not been formally established. But we need to think big, and have these strategic discussions now, rather than waiting until it is too late.

Even if this new project is free from the constraints of the Labour Party, it will still have to operate within the narrow confines of the British state. It will be disadvantaged by the first-past-the-post electoral system and Westminster's highly centralised political structures, both of which have previously stifled the left's attempts to develop a popular, independent platform. Shouldn't it therefore take explicit aim at these antidemocratic obstacles, advocating electoral reform and the breakup of the union as key parts of its agenda?

The case for proportional representation (PR) is getting more powerful as the political system fragments. We are now looking at five-party politics in England and six-party politics in Scotland and Wales, so PR should clearly be on the agenda of the next Parliament, and I think the new party should champion it. Even if it brings its own set of problems, they are clearly preferable to sticking with the present arrangement. Then again, nothing is going to change before the next election, which will have to be fought on first-past-the-post, so that will condition some of the immediate decisions that the new party has to make: about where it can win majorities and which seats it plans to prioritise.

The union is a trickier problem. A majority in the labour movement, and even in the Labour Party, have swung in favour of electoral reform; but there are still deep divisions among workers and socialists over the future of the multinational state itself. So here I think the new party has to be guided by its members in Scotland and Wales, who may of course come to different conclusions. It was my view in 2019 that Labour should have adopted the position that if the next Scottish Parliament had a majority in favour of a further independence referendum, following the defeat of the previous one in 2014, then it would be wrong to stand in its way. This was one of the few issues on which I think we had a democratic deficit, and I hope the new party will set that right by establishing structures that allow a legitimate policy decision to be made. But I think that's some way off at present.

You said that politics must be the first priority, ahead of organisational questions. But it isn't necessarily straightforward to come up with an abstract conception of the politics that will hold together all the disparate groups on the left, from the independent MPs to tenants' unions to existing socialist parties. Given this fractured situation, isn't the priority to figure out what kind of organisation would allow these forces to cohabit, so that they can then decide collectively on their programme?

That is true to a degree. Policies can only be determined in a democratic forum, presumably the founding conference due to be held this autumn. That will hopefully put the party on a firm footing and determine its first positions, if not an

exhaustive list of them, as well as adopting an initial consti-
tution. So yes, we have to start by taking some structural
steps. We need to find a way to organise these 750,000 people,
presumably on some geographical basis, so they can have an
input: perhaps an electronic voting system, perhaps a series
of more localised meetings or both. But we don't at this
point need a full elaboration of exactly how the organisation
will work or how it will deal with all these inevitable challenges. I am somewhat agnostic, for example, on the question of electoral alliance versus a party. A loose version of
the former could fail to articulate a coherent politics, while a
tightly centralised version of the latter could struggle to
draw in independent forces; we need something that's able to
do both. What I think most of the prospective members
want, along with the wider public, is a clear sense of where
the party stands. Some of them will remember Corbyn's
Labour leadership and see that as a reference point, but
others may not. Some will know that the party is left wing,
but they may not have a set of clear associations with this
term. So we need to set out our socialist orientation. There
will be a spectrum of views, of course, but they can be incor-
porated into this anti-systemic framework.

*What is the social basis of the new party? In his interview,
James Schneider proposes that the three non-mutually
exclusive categories of asset-poor workers, downwardly
mobile graduates and racialised communities could make up
a possible electoral majority.*

There is no doubt that we need an alliance that can win in
Bristol and Birmingham and East London and Brighton, and
have an impact in Burnley and Barnsley too, respecting the
different social compositions of those places. Towards that

end, you can obviously make an argument for different types of electoral targeting, where you look at the size of, say, the Muslim community in a particular constituency. But when it comes to our political vision and strategy, I'm not really in favour of this disaggregation of the working class, which often seems like it's only a few steps away from talking about 'Worcester woman' and 'Mondeo man'. I don't see the value of using terms like 'asset-poor workers', for instance. The defining feature of the working class is that it lives by selling its capacity for wage labour; none of it survives on assets alone. We should aim to be a working-class party, and we should not submit to the political fragmentation of the working class by forever slicing and dicing it sociologically.

James makes a number of strong arguments in his interview, but when it comes to this point there is a certain paradox, because he starts off by saying that we must pursue a strategy of electoral 'density', in which we run election campaigns in places where these three groups are numerically preponderant. But then he goes on to suggest that winning elections should not be among the main priorities of the new party: that its foremost concern should be building 'popular power' as opposed to parliamentary power. I'm not sure he quite reconciles these two positions.

The argument, as I understand it, is that the party should be a lever for a popular mobilisation. That is to say, it should both strengthen existing working-class institutions and set about creating new ones, so as to lay the civic foundations for contesting elections. What do you think of this general approach?

What James is talking about, although he doesn't use the phrase, is the reconstitution of the working class as a class for itself. I don't underestimate the central importance of this. The *Communist Manifesto* enjoins socialists to first of all organise the proletariat as a class – and this task clearly needs recapitulating. The old organisations and institutions, both formal ones within the labour movement and informal ones within communities, have been broken apart over the past forty years. Reversing this, even partially, is an imperative for moving towards socialism. But whether one should overburden the new party with this as an executive responsibility, as opposed to framing and articulating the project, is another question. My view is that by articulating a strident class politics – by taking that message into elections, into Parliament, into the media and the public sphere – we will already be helping that process of reconstitution. We will diffuse the idea that there is a coherent class project that could rescue society from its present depredations, without which the idea of a class for itself is meaningless. And that will have cascading political effects.

Popular mobilisations don't necessarily require the leadership of a new party. The Gaza movement did not have a party apparatus behind it, yet it has brought hundreds of thousands of people out on the streets of London every few weeks for a year and a half, as well generating intense local activity. Mobilisations of this kind tend to develop organically. If there is a need for them, working people will find a way to articulate it. You can't have figures from the party telling them to get active if they do not already feel that need. A potential unintended outcome of viewing the party as a vector for social movements is that it ends up assuming leadership of everything that's stirring in the progressive undergrowth – which is a capacity that it simply doesn't have. You would then end up with a cod-Leninism in a party not ideologically equipped for such an undertaking.

Of course, there is an important role for socialists to play in such movements. Take Stop the War as an example: we brought together organisers from different traditions – Communist, Trotskyist, Labour – and established a unified structure that helped to give shape and purpose to the mass resistance to the Iraq War. Had we not done so, that resistance may have been more fragmented, with different blocs of Muslims and pacifists and trade unionists going in separate directions. But the crucial point is that the movement would have happened anyway. It was always going to emerge in some form because the urgency was great enough. Socialists can shape struggles but not suck them out the end of their thumbs.

The party needs to act as a force of opposition at every point of effective political intervention. Make no mistake, the party should stay very close to mass movements. While Starmer is telling his MPs 'Don't go on picket lines!' our party should be saying 'You must go on picket lines!' Its local branches should associate with the Palestine solidarity movement, with housing campaigns, with pensioners' groups. I'm not presenting my view as the opposite to James's. But I think that the translation of these multiple struggles into a single party form would be very challenging. And I don't think we should see this as a prerequisite for fighting elections and promoting our politics at the highest level. While the hope is to make the working class a much more powerful social actor, we must also think about what is possible and doable at this initial stage.

Would the same argument apply to the trade unions, or would you put them in a different category to, say, the Palestine movement when it comes to their relationship with the new party?

In the short term I don't see the trade unions, as collective bodies, having a formal relationship to the new party. Obviously, vast numbers of trade unionists have signed up, which could have a positive influence on the politics of the labour movement; and members of the new party should of course be encouraged to get active in the unions: indeed, one immediate outcome of this founding process will likely be that people who are currently not engaged in the labour movement become engaged. But the idea that we should replicate the erstwhile, often caricatured strategy of the Communist Party – bringing together party members who belong to a given union in a sort of conclave and directing them to follow a particular line – does not seem practical. Later down the line, if the Starmer government continues to flounder, and if the new party is run properly, then we may see the unions moving away from one and towards the other. In which case we could think about the precise lineaments of that institutional connection.

It's ironic that a more movementist view of the party's purpose threatens to shade into Leninism, since it could mean imposing centralised direction on various popular struggles. And, conversely, a more Leninist perspective – which foregrounds the party's electoral leadership – is at risk of becoming movementist, because it relies on the idea that effective popular struggles will simply happen spontaneously, or 'organically', to use your word.

It's not that the strategy of effecting class regeneration through a range of different organisational forms is wrong, but I struggle to see the new party being able to make that an effective priority. I remember McDonnell and Jon Lansman and others sitting in my office in the Unite building in 2015 and talking about how they wanted Momentum to be a social movement. My response was that Momentum's necessary role was to defend Jeremy inside the Labour Party. It ended up doing that pretty effectively, and made a powerful intervention in the 2017 election. It never became a social movement because that wasn't the political imperative in those circumstances. As for Leninism: that requires a much higher degree of ideological militancy and unity from the outset than we are likely to get with this new party. I feel we are several stops short of democratic centralism right now.

If we're talking about how the party can make the most effective electoral interventions, then its leadership model is important. What is your view on that?

Any discussion at this stage will be provisional until a conference or a leadership election is held to settle the question democratically. But the organising committee that was established to try to drive this process forwards considered various leadership possibilities, including Jeremy as interim leader along with deputies, and Jeremy co-leading with Zarah Sultana. A majority voted for the latter, which is where my sympathies would lie. Of course, no one can make people co-leaders if they don't want to be co-leaders, so this depends on the active assent of the individuals concerned. But Jeremy and Zarah are clearly complementary. Their politics are the same. Their personal characteristics, their approaches to the project, the way they intervene in Parliament, the issues they prioritise: they are aligned on all these fronts. So this seems like the most forward-looking approach. On the left we often say that we can't pretend it's still 1917, but nor can we pretend it's still 2017 either. No one can rationally wish to rerun the 2015–19 experience. Honour the past, face the future.

Many of the international examples that are often cited as models for the British left have limited applicability. The UK's comparatively weak traditions of popular struggle suggest that it would find it difficult to develop anything resembling the most successful parties of the Pink Tide; its parliamentary system and political balance of forces mean that any left-wing electoral alliance wouldn't function like La France Insoumise; it lacks the social base to establish a vehicle like the Belgian Workers' Party . . .

Everyone on the left is still trying to find a route to socialism that is neither simply electing a parliamentary majority nor storming the Winter Palace. And, unfortunately, we have very few historical examples of how one actually does that: what combination of mass pressure, parliamentary work, organic struggle and perhaps some form of coercive power actually gets you over the line. The new party needs to open up a space where these questions – which were very much alive in the 1970s but have since slipped off everyone's radar – can be considered.

Fortunately, we do have a wealth of negative examples to avoid repeating. With Syriza, we saw a political explosion that led to the rapid formation of a government led by the new left, which soon ended in ignominy when it capitulated to the EU, reproducing the problems of classical Greek social democracy rather than transcending them. Podemos was weakly rooted from the beginning; it was described as having been launched by two corridors of professors from Complutense University. When it became the minority part-ner in a social-democratic-led government, it learned that, without deep social bases, it really couldn't make the weather. In Germany, the left split partly along culture war lines, although more substantive questions of war, Palestine and migration also separated Die Linke from the BSW. Its division has greatly diminished its political influence. So there are a number of ways in which European left parties have shown the path to ruin: by capitulation to monopoly capital, by a failure to embed themselves in the working class, by fracturing over particular issues like imperialist war and migration.

The Workers' Party in Belgium is interesting. When I first knew them they were still followers of Mao, but that has not proved a barrier to their advance. There is a lot to be studied in how they manage to unite parliamentary, community and trade union struggles. But each of these parties is *sui generis*, and ours will be too. I mean, five out of its initial six-person parliamentary group are Muslims; its very existence is a product of previous mass movements, its connection to the current ones is strong; and it draws on Corbyn's leadership of Labour – so we need to start from these particular defining features.

4

Britain After Gaza

Leanne Mohamad

Leanne Mohamad is a British-Palestinian activist. Born in 2000, she grew up in the town of Ilford, East London, and became a prominent advocate of Palestinian rights when she was a teenager. A community organiser and youth worker in her local area, she was active in student politics while studying at King's College London and joined the mobilisation against the Gaza genocide shortly after her graduation, addressing rallies of hundreds of thousands of people. In 2024 she was selected as the independent candidate for Ilford North, where she ran an insurgent campaign against the incumbent right-wing Labour MP and shadow health secretary Wes Streeting, who has been widely touted as a possible future prime minister. On election day Mohamad defied all expectations by coming within 528 votes of winning, a major embarrassment for the incoming government. She is now polling far ahead of Streeting in the constituency and would beat him with a projected margin of almost 4,000 votes in a new ballot.

OLIVER EAGLETON: *What is your background? How were you politicised?*

LEANNE MOHAMAD: My grandparents were among the 750,000 Palestinians who were forcibly expelled from their homeland by Zionist militias in 1948. Like many others, they thought it would be a matter of days, weeks or maybe months before they were able to return. But instead they ended up as refugees in Lebanon and were never allowed to go back. When I was growing up in Ilford, where I've spent almost my entire life, I heard their stories and felt their pain from a very young age. This was a living history that was passed down to me, not just through words but through our everyday life, as a family that was still scattered across the world because of occupation and the Nakba. I went to see the refugee camp that my father grew up in, which made this collective experience feel personal. It made politics feel urgent.

Most Palestinians don't have the privilege of growing into political awareness. We are born into it. We are politicised before we can even read. It's not as if we have a choice about whether to be engaged or disengaged; we are forced to confront Israeli oppression as a matter of necessity. Because I grew up in such a relatively privileged place, I always felt I needed to use my voice for justice. My faith played a huge part in that as well: it pushes you to act as soon as you see something that's wrong.

When I was fifteen my English teacher at secondary school nominated me to take part in the world's largest public speaking competition for young people. I was very shy at school and surprised to be asked – but she convinced me to do it, and I decided to speak about the issue that was most important to me: Palestine. My basic message was that

Palestinians are human beings, and their plight is a stain on humanity. I won the competition's regional final, and the video of my speech went viral, which was when the hate started: first as a trickle, then a deluge. The school's Twitter account was bombarded with abuse and had to be shut down. There were articles written about me in local papers and in the right-wing press. I was called antisemitic, a suicide bomber, an 'ISIS girl', a terrorist recruiter who needed to be burned alive. Because I was wearing my uniform in the video, people knew where I went to school, which was a huge safety concern. When the police were called, they just told me to shut down my social media accounts and keep quiet.

It was a scary episode, but it was also a formative one, and I'm grateful for the lesson it taught me, which is that you should never succumb to intimidation. They tried everything to silence me, but this meant that my voice travelled even further and reached a much wider audience. When I stood my ground, I received overwhelming support from friends and family and from people I had never met. The hashtag #LetLeanneSpeak went viral. I started to get invitations to speak on panels, at protest rallies, in Parliament. I found that I could draw on the experience of my grandparents, whose pain had given them an amazing resilience.

Ever since then, I've remained politically active and brushed off this kind of abuse. When I went to study at King's I got involved in the National Union of Students and I also became president of the Students for Justice in Palestine Society. Then, when the genocide in Gaza began in 2023, it made clear that the Nakba my family experienced wasn't an isolated event; it's a structure of violence that remains in place today, whose most destructive chapter is currently unfolding. The settler colonial project wants to make it as difficult as possible for anyone to oppose this horror. But if you're silent in the face of it, then you're an indirect participant, and that's something that most people in my community are not willing to be.

How has the assault on Gaza changed the politics of your generation?

This is the first time we've seen a genocide livestreamed on people's phones. The images are shocking and unbearable, but they're also a sign of something much bigger. The hypocrisy of the political class has never been clearer, as the British government approved licences for the munitions that are being dropped on innocents. Young people across the world are waking up to this and freeing themselves from a system that has polluted our air, our politics, our minds and our souls. Gaza ignited a passion in us that will be hard to extinguish. It's not just about fighting for Palestine; it's about fighting for humanity, against domination, racism and imperialism.

The tools that are normally used to get people to accept the status quo won't work. No one trusts the corporate media anymore; we've watched it try to stifle anyone who speaks the truth. No one believes in the two-party system, which forces people to choose the 'lesser of two evils' until there's nothing left but evil. The charade of difference between red and blue governments is meaningless when both of them support war abroad and treat people here at home with the same callousness: dividing communities against one another, letting public services fall into decay. We have no time for this stale duopoly which tries to restrict our political appetites.

Gaza has revealed the stark realities of life, and now that we've seen them, a lot of us will never be the same again. I became a Labour member when I was seventeen years old and Jeremy Corbyn was still leader, but when I heard Keir Starmer say that Israel had the right to cut off fuel and water to 2.2 million people, I resigned from the party immediately. My local community erupted with anger at our MP, Wes Streeting, who was then the shadow health secretary, because he refused to vote for a ceasefire. It became apparent to everyone that he simply wasn't willing to listen to the people he claimed to represent.

The movement against the genocide has taught us so much: not only about our broken politics, but also about what we really value. We don't want to be the kind of generation that sits by while other people suffer. We are looking beyond our immediate comforts and thinking about what we truly owe one another. This is a turning point in history.

Your campaign in Ilford North came within inches of kicking Streeting out of Parliament. You are now polling well ahead of him. Can you tell us about the area and the election?

Ilford North is the place that welcomed my parents and gave them a home when they arrived here as migrants. I still live there today, and naturally I care deeply about the welfare of my friends and neighbours. I've seen their problems first-hand as a local youth worker and a food bank volunteer. It's clear that many working-class people and pensioners are struggling to stay afloat while energy companies make record profits. It was because of that, and because of the mass outrage over Gaza, that a community group came together in 2024 and decided to recruit a candidate to run as an independent. One of its members approached me and asked if I would ever consider running as an MP. My response was, 'What do you mean, run as an MP?' I didn't even know it was possible to stand without a party machine behind you. But I asked for more details, and they showed me the numbers which proved that this seat was actually winnable. I was still confused about why they'd chosen me given that I was so young, but I remember thinking I might as well give it a try, since I would at least learn something from the experience.

Around twenty candidates ended up applying. We submitted statements, made short videos and did interviews. There was a long list, a short list, and then the final three participated in a hustings which was attended by two hundred people. The other contenders were much older and more experienced. We were all asked quick-fire questions by the host and then by the audience. It was probably the most stressful thing I'd ever done. During a break I saw the head of the youth centre that I went to when I was growing up and where I used to work, and I said to him, 'Oh my god, I just keep waffling on without knowing what I'm even saying!' He said, 'No, Leanne, people love your passion, they want something new from politicians – keep going!' Which made me think, you know what, I'll just continue to do my thing and see what happens. And in the end, when the people there voted to nominate a candidate, I got the most support. A week later I was called by someone in the community group who told me I'd been officially selected.

I couldn't really believe it was happening, and I felt a huge sense of responsibility because my community was counting on me. It was always going to be an uphill battle. The electoral system is stitched up to ensure that only two parties have a realistic chance of winning – which allows all kinds of vacuous careerists to make their way into Parliament, with the help of donations from lobbyists and big business. These politicians do their best to discourage any form of civic engagement and keep their constituents politically passive.

In Ilford North we not only have this dynamic; we also have a major national figure as our MP. Even if he couldn't win on a wave of popular enthusiasm, he would benefit from low turnout and deep resentment towards the Conservatives. On top of that, our campaign suffered from a complete media blackout, no political infrastructure and limited time to build it given the snap election. Lots of people thought that a young Muslim woman in a hijab was never going to make any headway. Some of them hoped we might decrease Labour's vote share by a couple thousand, but that was the extent of their ambition.

I knew that this was going to be a two-horse race between me and Labour, though, and that we had a good chance of unseating Streeting – because I knew how many other people like me were ready to fight back against the neglect of our community, and that we were going to do that by developing a method of campaigning that was entirely new for Ilford North. It was deeply embedded in the area; it was focused and strategic; it was people-powered; and above all, it had heart. I had a team that was immensely dedicated and a campaign manager who built an extremely professional and well-organised operation. Local people already knew me because of my community work, and there was a basic level of trust in someone who actually comes from the area, as opposed to a candidate who's parachuted in by a Westminster party.

I didn't want to dictate the main issues of the election. I wanted to listen to the constituents themselves. So that's what we did: we went out on the doorstep, asked people what they most cared about and how they thought we could effect change, and the campaign was shaped by them. Its themes came from the bottom up, from thousands of conversations and reams of data that we collected. The most widespread concerns turned out to be health, crime, education, youth services, the cost of living and foreign policy. The message I heard constantly was that the two-party system was not delivering. There was a very deep, very disturbing sense of betrayal: a frustration with flip-flopping between the same groups of self-serving politicians, neither of which has done anything to improve people's lives. That's why so many people were willing to turn to an independent alternative.

We assembled an inspiring, selfless and active group of volunteers, who gave everything to the campaign: days, nights, weekends. They showed up every single morning with nothing but belief. We delivered endless leaflets and stayed up late organising. Most of my support base were former Labour voters, but a considerable number were ex-Tories, who were willing to switch when they realised that there was a candidate who would genuinely put the interests of the community first. We gathered people of all faiths, all colours, all ethnicities. Local businesses also played their part, put up my posters, distributed my leaflets and even offered free meals to people who were wearing my volunteer T-shirts. Bringing these different groups together under the banner of humanity, at a time when Labour and the Tories were both fuelling the onslaught against the defenceless Palestinian population, was incredible. It gave us the ability to engage with everyone in every ward. We didn't leave any patch untouched across the whole community. I sat in people's front rooms and spoke about everything that was going on in their lives. I still remember every one of these conversations – people saying to me, 'Leanne, I've never voted before in my life, but this time I will.'

On election day we started seeing queues at polling stations stretching down entire streets. Volunteers were coming back to the campaign headquarters and telling me that something extraordinary was happening. It was emotional and it was exhausting. What we were seeing, in real time, was the end of the two-party nightmare. The result was going to be on a knife-edge. Streeting must have been sweating. I finally got to the election count in the early hours of the morning, and the outcome was announced around 3 a.m. Labour got 15,647 votes and I got 15,119: a margin of 528, or 1.1 per cent. Even though everything was stacked against us, we ended up shaking the establishment to its core. We almost ejected one of the Labour's most prominent frontbenchers and created major problems for his ambition to become prime minister. We did it because our campaign was not rooted in empty promises but in real people. More than just a campaign, it was a vision of the future, and it turned the page on the politics of the past.

How do we make sure that the energy generated by these insurgent campaigns doesn't dissipate before the next election? How can the new left party harness it?

The main aim here should be to keep communities together and keep their momentum going. It's easy to succumb to despair when the genocide has been happening for two years now and it feels like there's nothing more we can do. But the movement against it, combined with the independent election campaigns of 2024, has created fearless and determined groups of people across the country who want to rupture the status quo. In Ilford North we're about to start hosting monthly public conversations on many different issues that matter to the community, bringing in various guest speakers, building local trust and accountability. This kind of accessible political education can help to explain how power works and how to challenge it. Because most people are so disconnected from established power they don't realise how much power they actually have. Right now the task is to turn their justified anger into something more sustained, more effective, and that relies on consistent organising: the development of local networks whose purpose is not just to support insurgent election campaigns but to create a collective agent and a political infrastructure that will outlast any individual candidate.

Islamophobia is not only a driving force behind the government's policy in the Middle East; it is also an increasingly central pillar of its domestic programme. What's the most effective means of combating it?

As a visibly Muslim woman this is something I have to deal with a lot. I've seen how much Islamophobia has been on the rise since the beginning of the genocide. People in my community have noticed a sharp increase in this kind of racism, thanks in part to figures like Farage, Trump and Musk, whose rhetoric often translates into direct violence, spreading from the online world onto the streets. We are currently living in a society where our children can be judged or targeted simply because of who they are. Changing this requires action on many different levels.

First of all, our communities should refuse to live in fear. We should not be intimidated, as I said earlier, nor should we retreat from politics in the face of this assault. By standing together as Muslims and non-Muslims, united in our opposition to Islamophobia, we can show that solidarity defeats hate. This means challenging the government at the level of policy, when its actions – overseas or domestic – discriminate against Muslims, as they so often do. At the level of society, meanwhile, we have to demand fair representation of

Muslims in spheres where they are routinely stigmatised, such as the media and academia. Narratives that normalise Islamophobia by presenting Muslims as 'security threats' rather than citizens need to be undermined wherever they appear. Again, popular education is critical: developing resources to raise awareness in areas where the official education system is wilfully failing. This can also take the form of multi-faith dialogue, bringing faith groups together to show them that Islamophobia isn't just a 'Muslim issue' but one of fundamental rights. Reshaping people's everyday vocabularies in this way can counter the racist paradigms that the press and politicians are trying to advance.

The base of the new left party spans Muslims with some socially conservative views and leftists who foreground social progressivism. How can we keep these groups together?

Both sides need to compromise with one another without compromising their values. For those in the Muslim community who are socially conservative, they've got to accept – and most of them do already accept – that one should not discriminate against others whatever one's personal beliefs. The vast majority of Muslims take that view in their daily lives; they are very tolerant towards everyone regardless of their identities. On the other side, social progressives have to recognise the true meaning of pluralism: that not everyone needs to conform to their outlook, that people are free to practise all kinds of beliefs. As a constituency MP and as a political leader, Corbyn has always embodied this type of pluralism. He may disagree with some members of his constituency on certain questions, he may not share all their values, but he doesn't set out to change them. Rather than seeing their social and religious views as a problem to be solved, he works to build a community where everyone can come together through their shared material interests, which are much stronger than the small number of issues on which there might be division. That's the approach that the new left party needs to take.

5

Lessons of Corbynism

Alex Nunns

Alex Nunns is an author and activist who worked as Jeremy Corbyn's speechwriter from 2018 to 2020. He has chronicled the ups and downs of the British left over the past decade for publications such as Jacobin *and* Red Pepper, *as well as editing books by Julian Assange and Norman Finkelstein, among others. His book* The Candidate *(2017) was widely acclaimed as the definitive account of Corbyn's rise to the top of the Labour Party and the broader conditions that enabled it. In his forthcoming work,* Sabotage *(2026), he analyses the establishment campaign that eventually toppled the socialist leadership, allowing Keir Starmer to reclaim the party for the right.*

OLIVER EAGLETON: *Why is the Corbyn project of 2015–19 relevant to the new left party?*

ALEX NUNNS: Your Party is being created against the backdrop of the Corbyn phenomenon. It's safe to assume most of the people who have signed up as supporters were shaped politically by the experience of Jeremy Corbyn's leadership of Labour. The lucky ones may even have made it though without lasting post-traumatic stress disorders. It was an intense and often bewildering period, and to learn its lessons we need a well-grounded understanding of what happened.

After the 2019 election, when Labour's defeat was fresh, the constraints that Jeremy and the movement had operated under could still be felt, and the overwhelming forces that had vanquished us remained visible. Some of that has since been forgotten. More recently, a simplistic reading of history has gained ground, which suggests that the defeat of the Corbyn project was self-inflicted through cowardice and timidity, including that of individual advisers or the leader himself. This line of thinking has a certain ironic affinity with the view of the Corbyn years presented in journalistic accounts like Gabriel Pogrund and Patrick Maguire's *Left Out* and Owen Jones's *This Land*, which place a comparable emphasis on office politics at the top of Labour. But whereas in those books the leadership tends to be characterised as too intransigent or radical to run an effective opposition, in this new reading the focus on key personalities is the same but the argument is inverted: Corbyn and his advisers were not defiant or radical enough. The fatal flaw in the Corbyn project, it's claimed, was the political weakness of its leading figures, who gave way instead of standing their ground.

This gets the story of Corbyn's Labour wrong. It ignores the larger structural factors that actually shape history and so neglects vital insights into what happens when a left party comes close to gaining power. The reality is that Corbyn and those around him spent five years fighting tooth and nail against far more powerful opponents, while being hampered throughout by a sabotage operation of unprecedented scale and intensity. They didn't surrender; they lost.

That said, the historically remarkable thing was not that Corbynism was defeated in 2019, but that it wasn't defeated until then. It vastly exceeded expectations on multiple fronts. It made austerity a dirty word, forced the Conservative government back on key policies, pushed the political conversation to the left, galvanised a movement, transformed Labour into the biggest left party in Europe and gave people hope. In the 2017 election Labour surged to 40 per cent of the vote, recording the biggest increase in vote share of any party since 1945. It won 12.9 million votes for a left platform – still Labour's second highest tally since 1966 – and gained seats for the first time in twenty years, depriving the Conservatives of their majority. The establishment wants to erase that from history. Let's not help them by rewriting the story as one of unremitting failure. There were mistakes and shortcomings, to be sure, but the new party can only learn from them if they are properly diagnosed.

You mentioned a sabotage operation. How did that work?

There were two distinct waves of sabotage. The first lasted from 2015–17 and was about who controlled the party. The second, from 2017–19, was about who controlled the country. To understand the first wave, bear in mind that the outer wall of the British establishment ran through the middle of the Labour Party. On one side were foot soldiers of the state and capital, who dominated the party's elected representatives and staff; on the other were socialists and radicals who had been kept out of positions of influence for most of Labour's history. When Jeremy won the leadership, he wasn't just taking the helm of a democratic party, he was storming one of the establishment's fortresses. The response was predictably fierce. Labour bureaucrats and parliamentarians undermined the leadership at every turn. Right-wing staff in Labour's HQ refined the art of bureaucratic obstruction and leaked to the press continuously. Meanwhile, MPs volunteered their services to the media to denounce virtually everything the leadership did, meaning that no matter what the issue was, the headlines were dominated by 'Labour division'. The Parliamentary Labour Party – the collective term for Labour MPs – made itself ungovernable.

This climaxed in the attempted coup of 2016, when MPs tried to force Jeremy to resign with coordinated resignations and a vote of no confidence. When he refused, making his opponents challenge him in a leadership election, the party bureaucracy tried to exclude him from the ballot but was foiled by the trade unions. It didn't stop there. In the 2017 election, Labour staff ran a secret parallel campaign, diverting party resources to their allies in safe seats in defiance of the ambitious offensive strategy agreed by the party's official campaign committee. In the end, the result was so close in crucial seats that it's possible to argue that if those resources had been allocated to the right constituencies, it could have toppled the Conservative government.

During this first wave of sabotage, the British establishment mostly relied on its allies in the Labour Party to neutralise the Corbyn leadership. It effectively said, 'You've landed yourself with this left-wing leader; it's your job to get rid of him. We'll leave it to you.' Happily, this kind of sabotage won't recur in the new party, at least not initially, because it won't have the same place in the British governing system. It will be entirely outside the fortress.

When Jeremy confounded everyone and came close to power in 2017, he became the biggest domestic threat to the British establishment since the aftermath of the First World War. This triggered the second wave of sabotage. Jeremy was

unassailable as Labour leader, so a more sophisticated operation, involving a wider cast of characters, was now needed
to stop him becoming prime minister. This effort was mostly
channelled through two long-running controversies – the
'Labour antisemitism crisis' and Brexit. Both deepened divisions within the party, including within the leadership itself,
and discredited it more widely. There are more lessons for
the new party here.

*It's worth looking at these two controversies more closely.
How was the antisemitism crisis concocted?*

When Jeremy became Leader of the Opposition, Britain
had, for the first time, a potential prime minister who was
unequivocally committed to Palestinian rights. This alone
mobilised a coalition of Israel supporters against him.
What followed was a concerted campaign that seized on
allegations of antisemitism against Labour members and
Jeremy himself to inflict maximum political damage on the
Corbyn leadership. This coalition encompassed the Labour
right, an Atlanticist tendency for whom support for Israel
had become a bizarrely prominent part of its identity, and
the associated Jewish Labour Movement and Labour
Friends of Israel; outside the party it extended to all the
pro-Israel Jewish communal organisations, such as the
Board of Deputies of British Jews and the Jewish Leadership
Council, plus the Jewish communal press; the full breadth
of the British establishment; and international actors
including the state of Israel itself, whose prime minister
Benjamin Netanyahu publicly condemned Corbyn, and the
US, whose secretary of state Mike Pompeo told Jewish
leaders in New York that Washington would do its 'level
best' to 'push back' against a Corbyn government. This

was a hugely powerful bloc. Most of its campaigning was channelled through a complicit media – including the BBC and the *Guardian* – which devoted credulous and dispro-portionate coverage to antisemitism claims while showing an unshakable lack of interest in the political agendas behind them.

While there evidently were some cases of Labour members making antisemitic comments, usually online, it's beyond doubt that, as Jeremy later put it, 'the scale of the problem was also dramatically overstated for political reasons by our opponents'. Morgan McSweeney, who's now Keir Starmer's chief of staff, was at the time trawling pro-Corbyn Facebook groups for antisemitic comments from random members of the public and feeding them to the *Sunday Times*. Yet despite his efforts, and those of a network of people doing similar work, only a tiny fraction of the membership was ever the subject of a complaint. But that was never really the point. The idea being pushed by those orchestrating the campaign was that the party leadership, its mass base and even left-wing ideas themselves were fundamentally and pervasively antisemitic. This was wholly false.

The story behind the infamous BBC *Panorama* documentary 'Is Labour Antisemitic?', broadcast just months before the 2019 general election, illustrates how this campaign worked. Initially, staff working in the party's complaints unit, who were hostile to the leadership, were extremely slow to process even clear-cut cases of antisemitism such as Holocaust denial – perhaps because they wanted the blame to fall on Jeremy, or perhaps because they were bafflingly incompetent bureaucrats. Some examples of these cases found their way into the press. Labour MPs demanded, 'Why won't Corbyn intervene?' A narrative was spun that Jeremy was failing to act on antisemitism.

By spring 2018 the left was finally strong enough to oust the right-wing general secretary of the party, Iain McNicol, and, during a hiatus of a few weeks before his successor took over, the staff in the complaints unit decided to ask the Leader's Office for advice on individual cases. These requests were generally met with encouragement to take action, with the exception of a handful of cases involving anti-Zionist Jewish members. The email exchanges, whose content was entirely uncontroversial, were later leaked to the media and ultimately formed the crux of the *Panorama* documentary by journalist John Ware, who had previously denounced Corbyn as 'stimulated by disdain for the West [and] appeasement of extremism'. His documentary suggested Labour staff had been hampered in dealing with antisemitism complaints due to interference from the Leader's Office.

The MPs now realised they had been saying the wrong thing. Instead of 'Why won't Corbyn intervene?' the call became 'How dare Corbyn interfere!' After the Equality and Human Rights Commission – an arm's-length body of the state, run by government appointees – launched an investigation into antisemitism in the Labour Party, these same allegations became one of the central planks of its report. The fanfare around the report's release in 2020 created a false impression that Jeremy had interfered to protect antisemites. The fact the evidence pointed the other way was politely ignored by all, and an attempt by Jeremy to push back even mildly against the fictitious notion that Labour had been overrun by antisemitism earned him suspension and ultimately exclusion from the party at the hands of his successor, Keir Starmer. So, there you have it: a sequence of events in which different parts of the establishment were effectively working in concert. Party bureaucrats associated with the

Labour right engage in inadvertent or deliberate obstruction; this gives ammunition to right-wing Labour MPs to attack the leadership; the claims get amplified by a hostile media and are ultimately weaponised by the state.

So how does this analysis relate to the new party? What can it learn, including negatively, from the Corbyn leadership's response to the smear campaign?

The campaign I've described obviously couldn't recur in the same form in the new party. One of the features that made it so difficult to respond to was the fact that much of it emanated from within the Labour Party itself, involving staff and MPs, many of whom had been engaged in the wider sabotage operation since 2015. Another feature of the campaign was its mobilisation of an identity politics that was then reaching its zenith on the left, making it very hard for left-wingers to dispute what people described as their 'lived experience' of racism.

Of course, the rest of that enormous coalition of powerful forces ranged against Corbyn's Labour will also mobilise against Your Party, especially if it comes close to power. So, it's understandable that some people would call for Your Party to be defiant and robust from the outset, in supposed contrast to the Corbyn leadership which is accused of having given too much ground. This was reflected by Zarah Sultana in her interview, when she said Corbynism 'capitulated' to the IHRA definition of antisemitism. But Jeremy didn't capitulate: on the contrary, he and his team held out to the bitter end in an attempt to resist the adoption by Labour's National Executive Committee (NEC) of the most problematic examples that accompany the IHRA definition – some of which have been used to clamp down on pro-Palestinian speech and Palestinians' right to describe their own dispossession. Jeremy endured hell throughout the summer of 2018 for making this stand; no other part of the Labour movement represented on the NEC stuck by him. Right down to the wire, at the NEC meeting in September 2018 when the examples were adopted in full, Jeremy tabled a statement arguing that it 'should not be regarded as antisemitic to describe Israel, its policies or the circumstances around its foundation as racist because of their discriminatory impact, or to support another settlement of the Israel-Palestine conflict' (that is, one state). There wasn't enough support to put it to a vote. There was no magic lever Jeremy or his team could pull to change that situation. The Labour Party is a byzantine organisation with multiple power centres; being the leader doesn't mean you can always get your way.

A more valid criticism of Corbynism would be that the organised parts of the project – including the leadership and the left-wing campaign group Momentum – didn't sufficiently shield grassroots members from the antisemitism firestorm. The mechanisms for two-way engagement with the broader movement were lacking. Some members who were wrongly accused of antisemitism suffered hugely traumatic experiences that changed their lives. It's easy to forget how suffocating the atmosphere was. It demoralised the movement. At the top level, while it's naïve to imagine that defiant statements from the leader would have stopped this concerted campaign, there could have been a greater effort, especially early on, to emphasise Jeremy's support for Palestinian rights as an explanation for the furore, which otherwise appeared baffling. If the same events were to occur today, that connection would be more obvious to people because of the genocide in Gaza. We're in a different context now.

And Brexit?

It's interesting that the antisemitism crisis now looms larger than Brexit in many people's minds, but it wasn't the cause of Corbynism's defeat. At the apex of the antisemitism crisis, in summer 2018, Labour remained at 40 per cent in the polls. The collapse only happened in 2019, especially around the European elections in May, by which time Brexit had become a political black hole, engulfing every other issue.

The dynamic of the sabotage in this case was different. Of course, Brexit was always going to split Labour's support base to some extent, but those divisions were deliberately exacerbated to harm the leadership. In the 2017 election an overwhelming majority had voted for parties committed to respecting the referendum vote to leave the European Union. But it wasn't long before the campaign for a second referendum – to overturn the first – was making inroads. Many supporters of the 'People's Vote' campaign and like-minded groups were earnest and passionate Remainers, but there was no mistaking that the organisations themselves tended to be steered by a kind of Blairite revival theatre troupe, including disgraced figures like Peter Mandelson and Alastair Campbell, with Tony Blair himself lurking backstage. Remainerism gave these washed-up actors a fresh audience and a new lease of life. They may have railed against a Tory Brexit, but the real target of their campaign was Corbyn's Labour: they saw an opportunity to drive a wedge between a leadership mindful that a majority of Labour constituencies had voted to Leave, and a party membership that mostly wanted to Remain. Much the same group of saboteur MPs who had tried to overrule the members' choice for leader a few years earlier now found themselves aligned with the members on an issue they could use to undermine the leadership.

This campaign crept up through the Parliamentary Labour Party like rising damp. It could be seen early on in performative amendments in Parliament. A small but telling example in November 2017 was an amendment to the Customs Bill to keep the UK in the EU single market and customs union, voted for by a core group of hostile right-wing Labour MPs. The amendment was economically 'illiterate', according to Labour's trade secretary Barry Gardiner, because it would have prevented the UK placing tariffs on any goods from anywhere in the world, but that didn't matter because the purpose was simply for the MPs to brief journalists like Robert Peston that Labour's front bench had shamefully voted with the Tories and betrayed the cause. Gradually, the number of parliamentarians involved in such operations grew, until the damp climbed to the level of the shadow cabinet. Starmer, then Corbyn's Brexit secretary, became the central figure, using media interviews and speeches to consistently and incrementally exceed the bounds of the leadership's position, most dramatically at the 2018 party conference, when he added an unapproved line to his speech announcing that Remain would not be ruled out as an option in a future referendum. It's plain from journalistic accounts that he was positioning himself to succeed Jeremy, and the fact he abandoned all his Remainer convictions as soon as he became leader gives an indication of how genuinely he held them.

By 2019, this damp had even reached the Leader's Office and Jeremy's inner circle. The leadership team became divided, with some of Jeremy's closest allies urging a more Remain position, including John McDonnell, Diane Abbott and policy director Andrew Fisher, while others like Karie

Murphy, Seumas Milne, Jon Trickett and Ian Lavery argued that Labour could not afford to abandon Leave voters. This was a disagreement about electoral strategy – John and co were not saboteurs; I'm sure they genuinely feared Labour would suffer catastrophic electoral consequences if it alienated Remain voters and its own activists. But with their view in the ascendant, the sabotage operation achieved its goal of manoeuvring the leadership into a hopeless position that split its coalition. Just as importantly, by swerving towards Remain, Jeremy no longer appeared as an insurgent outsider, but rather another politician defending the status quo, on the same side as the bulk of the establishment.

In your account, then, the problem with Corbynism was not internal weakness but external pressure. But are these two things incompatible? Wasn't it the case that, as a result of the sabotage operation, certain politicians and advisers ended up taking compromise positions – most notably on Brexit – which turned out to be strategically disastrous?

You have to take it issue by issue. On Brexit it wasn't the weakness of politicians and advisers but rather a split between them over strategy. The matter was never really resolved: the Brexit policy that the party ended up with at the 2019 election was a fudge that reflected the balance of forces. A significant factor was that Jeremy is a genuine democrat, who was subject to countervailing democratic pressures. He wanted to honour the popular vote for Leave, and he also cared that most Labour members and voters were demanding a second referendum. His efforts to reflect these different democratic demands goes some way towards explaining the party's final policy.

But isn't it fair to characterise the Brexit debacle as a situation in which some of the prime movers of Corbynism – at different points in time and to varying degrees – buckled under establishment pressure and made concessions that undermined the project? If this is the case, then Sultana's argument that the new left party needs to avoid the mistakes of the past by taking a more combative stance towards its class enemies would seem potentially useful. Or, to put it another way, if Corbynism was always beset by the contradiction between an antagonistic strategy ('for the many, not the few') and a more pacifist one ('kinder, gentler politics'), the proposal that Your Party should now choose the first over the second could have a galvanising effect on its members. By contrast, your emphasis on the 'balance of forces' as the explanation for Corbynism's unhappy ending might come across as defeatist, since that balance has hardly tilted in our favour in 2025. It might suggest that there's nothing we can do to change this vast power asymmetry.

Not capitulating to class enemies is a very good idea. Your Party should be antagonistic towards them. But I don't think we should console ourselves with a false history that says that if only Corbyn had been more combative then things would have turned out well. It's true that the Corbyn leadership was beset by the contradiction you outline: trying to practise left-populism while also presiding over one of the two established Westminster parties. Corbynism worked best when it was a disruptive outside force, as it was in 2017, and it's worth criticising certain tactics that strayed from that approach. But that isn't the only lesson we should draw.

Working in the Labour Party was both a blessing and a curse. For most of the 2015–19 period, wrestling for control of the party meant we had to fight on two fronts, but it also imposed a certain discipline on the movement. Everyone pulled together to take on the internal enemy, the Labour right. The new movement, with its own party, won't have that glue to bind it. What's more, in the Labour years Downing Street looked like a prize that was almost within reach. Running a 'party of government' meant we had to develop a broad left platform that would appeal to a wide swathe of the population.

The removal of the constraints imposed by working in the Labour Party will be hugely liberating for the left in the years to come, but it will also create a different set of problems. I don't think there's much danger of the new party being too conciliatory or weak-willed. On the contrary, it's more likely to be susceptible to demand inflation – where the most radical demands win, leading to competition over who can be most radical, until an effective class-based programme with mass appeal is subsumed by political positions which, though sincerely and passionately held, divide our movement and reduce our potential support. This is where leadership plays an important role. Leaders can have a strategic overview of where the party should position itself to succeed and convince the members to follow them. But if Jeremy or Zarah or any other leading figure were to play into the demand-inflation spiral, then the party could be overrun by internecine conflict before it's even founded.

We have to set our ambitions high. We should be aiming to replace the Labour Party and ultimately take power. The crises we're facing, which are only going to intensify, require nothing less. So we need to put forward a popular programme that can win power, without compromising our principles. In 2017 Corbyn's Labour did very well on a class-based 'for the many, not the few' platform. In 2019 it was defeated when Brexit, a cross-class issue, cut our coalition and our movement in two. That's an example to keep in mind.

The new party is still going to come under vicious attack, from without if not necessarily from within. How do you think this will differ from the Corbyn period?

Any left party that makes serious gains will face a backlash from capital, the state and the media. But it won't take the same form as last time. On the upside, it's much easier to deal with purely external attacks that don't involve internal sabotage or division. Remember the *Sun*'s claim in 2018 that Jeremy had been a communist spy working for Czechoslovakia? They really thought it was going to finish him. But the story didn't rely on the Labour right, nor did they make much use of it. The leadership was able to bat it away in straightforward populist terms, casting Jeremy as an underdog, a victim of smears by the powerful. It helped that he's a very implausible spy. If Your Party could choose the attacks it receives, it would choose this kind, where they can be turned around to illustrate the party's anti-establishment credentials.

In most of the world, throughout most of history, the path to power for left parties has been blocked by obstacles that turned out to be insurmountable: the imbalance of resources, the hostility of institutions and so on. The new party will have to contend with those head on. One advantage of being in the Labour Party was that we were already halfway over those hurdles: we had resources, our relevance was not in question, and parts of the British power structure had to at least contemplate coming to terms with us, in case we became the government. On the other hand, being in the

Labour Party mandated a heavy focus on electoralism rather than movement politics, which is an area where the new project might have more success – although building power outside Parliament is bound to be a slow and difficult process.

You say that the priority at this moment is to manage internal party conflicts and form a majoritarian programme. Is this compatible with full, member-led democracy? And is it achievable without a wider political culture of mass popular participation? The lack of that culture is surely part of the reason why Corbynism struggled to fight back against sabotage.

It's very hard to see how this new party could be set up without inclusive democratic structures. That's what Jeremy believes in and always has done given his Bennite influences. It's also what Zarah believes in. And it's what the huge numbers who have signed up to Your Party expect. That's something to be excited about. To make this work, the nascent party needs to nurture a culture of pluralistic debate where divisive issues can be negotiated, especially while the party is in its infancy. When it comes to crafting a programme that can appeal to a majority, I suspect the more people involved the better.

As for the broader question about Britain's political culture, you're right that Corbynism as a whole didn't have the depth and strength it needed to weather the onslaught. When Jeremy was Labour leader, the long-term erosion of the party's organic roots in the working class – not just the trade unions but all the social bases of working-class politics – was a cause of despair. Ironically, the acceleration of that process makes it far more plausible that Starmer's Labour – now languishing at around 20 per cent in the polls, having failed to win as many votes as Jeremy did in 2017 or 2019 – could be swept away, allowing a new force on the left to replace it. The task then will be to make sure Your Party sets down roots of its own, to avoid being swept away in turn. That is the goal. The opportunity is there.

6

A New Politics

Andrew Feinstein

Andrew Feinstein is a South African campaigner, author and politician. He was born in 1964 to a Cape Town family actively engaged in the liberation struggle and joined the African National Congress (ANC) at an early age. Forced to leave the country in his twenties, he studied at Berkeley and Cambridge and was preparing for a career as a psychoanalyst when the apartheid system began to falter. Upon returning home, he was elected as an ANC MP under Nelson Mandela's presidency, serving first in the Gauteng Provincial Legislature and then in the lower house of Parliament.

At the turn of the century, Feinstein – now tasked with overseeing South Africa's public finances – collided head-on with the ANC government when he tried to investigate a corrupt, multibillion-dollar arms deal that the party was intent on signing. He left the country and settled in Camden, where he has lived ever since, working as the director of Shadow World Investigations, a research outlet that exposes the effects of the global weapons trade. His books include After the Party *(2007), which documents his disillusionment with the ANC, and two pathbreaking works on the arms industry:* The Shadow World *(2012) and* Monstrous Anger of the Guns *(2024).*

In the 2024 election Feinstein challenged Keir Starmer for the seat of Holborn and St Pancras, running a community-led campaign that massively reduced the Labour leader's vote share, which fell by more than 17 per cent. Since then, Feinstein has established the Camden People's Alliance to campaign on local issues, as well as being heavily involved in discussions about the new left party.

OLIVER EAGLETON: *Can you start by telling us about your background in the ANC? How did you become involved in the movement against apartheid and how does it affect your outlook on the present political moment?*

ANDREW FEINSTEIN: My dad was South African and my mum was Austrian. She was a Holocaust survivor, and she met my dad in the UK before moving to South Africa with him. When she arrived there, her immediate impression was that the majority of South Africans were being treated much like the Jews of Europe had been treated. My dad had been peripherally involved in a group called the Congress of Democrats, which was a predominantly white affiliate of the ANC in the years before it was banned in 1955. My mum got active in a human rights organisation called the Black Sash, and she also worked at a non-racial theatre, as she was a puppeteer by profession. So, I grew up in an environment where I was mixing with very politicised and progressive people from a young age. During my school holidays I'd either be at the theatre, where there were all sorts of extraordinary anti-apartheid playwrights and actors and musicians, or I would be in the townships, which was very unusual at the time; in 1994 less than 0.4 per cent of white South

Africans had ever visited a black township. My family also moved around a lot. My dad would sometimes get home on a Friday and say, 'I can't live in this place anymore,' and the following Monday we would move continents, so I spent time in Austria and Britain and Holland, which exposed me to other societies that weren't as dysfunctional.

Given all this, it felt natural to get engaged in township politics. My first involvement was in the welfare and development field, where I ran an organisation at the University of Cape Town that provided education and health clinics in black townships and in the Cape Flats. Through this work I came into contact with the ANC when it was still illegal. I was invited to meetings that I didn't realize at the time were underground ANC gatherings, and I met some people who would go on to play significant roles in our first government.

After a spell in the UK and the US, where I moved to avoid military conscription, I started working as a facilitator in the constitutional negotiations and in various other transitional processes once the ban on the ANC was lifted. Then, while I was in Bangladesh getting married in late 1993, I saw that the party had released their lists of candidates for the various legislatures in the 1994 elections, and my name was on it. So, I dived straight into the campaign and was elected to the Gauteng Provincial Legislature. After about a year, Nelson Mandela moved me to the national Parliament, where I worked mainly on financial accountability and the Public Accounts Committee. Later, under President Thabo Mbeki, my committee tried to investigate a very large, very corrupt arms deal, and we were blocked, which led to a huge falling out between me and the government. I resigned the night before they were going to kick me out of Parliament.

The relevance of this potted history to the present moment in Britain lies in the experience of anti-apartheid activism. The crucial thing about that time is that the liberation movement was an incredibly broad front. There were lots of small, ideologically driven groups – especially in Cape Town – and initially there were major divisions between them: the Pan Africanist Congress broke away from the ANC around the issue of whites' role in the struggle, for example. But by the time the movement reached its apex in the late 1980s, it managed to incorporate everyone across the political spectrum who opposed the system, from Thatcherite neoliberals to revolutionary Marxists to anarcho-syndicalists. This was partly because the intensity of the state repression caused people to put those differences aside and focus on achieving a unified set of objectives for the first stage of liberation.

This is something that continues to influence my politics, particularly when I think about the new party. I didn't grow up on the British left; I was formed by a very different set of conditions which taught me the importance of broad-church politics. So, when people here bring up longstanding ideological disputes and try to exclude certain people on the basis that they are historically associated with this or that political tendency, I find it quite strange. My view is: Why can't we put that behind us and try to find the common ground for an inclusive, progressive alliance? In South Africa we focused on the issues that united us. Even though we're now in a very different historical situation, I think this lesson still holds, not least because of the depth of the crises that we're facing and the increasingly repressive character of the British state. The fact that more than 800,000 people have already signed up for the new party shows there is a basis for a mass politics of the left: a broad set of values that cuts across even fairly significant differences on individual issues.

In one sense it seems self-evident that a broad church is what's needed right now. But in another sense, isn't the aim to reject the broach-church politics of Labourism and allow the left to assert itself as an independent political force? How do we make sure that the parameters of our coalition are both wide enough to be effective and narrow enough to be coherent?

The right wing of the Labour Party has never been a broad church. In the early days of Blairism there was a perception that the Labour government was attempting to bring the left into the fold, but it soon became clear that this would only happen if the left adhered entirely to its Blairite political programme. That has more or less been the case ever since. Over the last three decades, though, the Labour right's definition of the left has also been constantly expanding, so that anyone who believes in basic social democratic principles, ideas that were once considered centrist, is now placed in this camp. Under Starmer, 'the left' has become a pejorative term for people who maintain some level of respect for civil liberties, for peace rather than war, for economic redistribution – all of whom should, in his view, be politically marginalised. That's a worrying development, but the upside is that these people, who form a clear majority in Britain, can come together as a political force. As establishment politics becomes narrower, the opposition becomes broader.

The South African example shows that a broad front is easier to assemble when you have a common enemy and a clear set of guiding principles. For the liberation movement, one of those principles was non-racialism: one person, one vote. That might sound like common sense in 2025, but that's partly because the campaign against apartheid helped to make it common sense. At the time, there were a number of 'liberal' groups that advocated for positions like democracy within the confines of a qualified franchise, so it was obvious that they could not be part of our coalition. Another essential principle was internationalism: solidarity with oppressed people elsewhere in the world, whose emancipation struggles mirrored ours.

Liberation movements take place in stages. In their initial phases, they need to be based on certain core principles which can coalesce different groups and actors. Later, they can get into the minutiae of a policy agenda and stake out a comprehensive set of positions. That is obviously necessary for creating a functional political party that can address a vast range of social problems. But I don't think we're quite there yet. Building a broad movement comes first.

You mentioned internationalism as a core principle. It strikes me that in the Holborn and St Pancras election you managed to mediate between various levels of politics: at once running a local campaign on issues like council services, a critic of Starmerism as a national project, and an opponent of the global order, whose moral bankruptcy is evident in the destruction of Gaza. How should the new party forge those connections between the local, the national and the international?

My day job is the main reason why those links are so obvious and so important to me. I research the global arms industry, looking at its economic logic, its trade networks, its corrupt practices and its destructive effects. While all this has been brought to the fore by the horrific events we've witnessed since October 7, it also goes much further than Palestine. Having spent a long time reading and writing about British militarism, I've become aware of the deep ties between domestic arms companies, the state and overseas governments. The arms deal I investigated in South Africa not only involved major bribes paid by BAE Systems; it also reached upward to the highest levels of government. Tony Blair made multiple visits to South Africa to ensure that BAE won a contract, even though the company didn't even meet the basic technical specifications. I then discovered that the corruption in these deals also funds the political parties and sometimes individual politicians in the selling countries too, corrupting the political systems of the buyers and sellers.

This collaboration between weapons makers and politicians is now deepening under Starmer, and it has a massive effect on people's everyday lives in Britain, in the following way. First of all, the vast majority of the money we spend on defence doesn't make us any safer; if anything, it is counterproductive. Britain has spent many billions of pounds on the F-35 jet, which an expert has described as 'the trillion-dollar turkey' because it simply isn't fit for purpose. This is a staggering economic opportunity cost. Second, the Labour government's plan to ramp up spending on armaments – taking it to unprecedented heights – means that other parts of the state are defunded. Defence companies are heavily subsidised by the public sector. We are on track for a £15.4 billion increase in the defence budget by the 2027 fiscal year, while an almost identical sum is being cut from the NHS and social welfare. It is important to make clear how these trade-offs work at both a national and a local level: how Britain's malfeasant role in the world deepens the cost-of-living crisis and destroys services that people desperately need. Of course, in the 2024 election, you could relate that explicitly to Gaza, where public funds are being used to wage a war that the overwhelming majority of Britons oppose. I don't believe that the UK government is simply enabling or facilitating that conflict. Like many other countries in the West, Britain is an active participant: sending arms which are used to massacre Palestinians and flying spy planes over Gaza to assist Israeli intelligence.

One tool that can be used to channel public anger about these issues is what we call a people's forum, meaning a local assembly where members of the community come to discuss certain issues and decide on a collective course of action. The ANC used this method in the run-up to the 1994 elections. In Holborn and St Pancras we were forced to run a very last-minute campaign, but we still managed to hold some people's forums where residents could draw connections between a number of different political questions – which is precisely how the continuities between the local and the international can begin to crystallise.

It is hard to overstate the importance of this type of community engagement. We knocked on more than 52,000 doors in my constituency, and initially the people working on my campaign would get frustrated because I'd often stop to have long conversations. But it soon became clear just how important it is to engage with people on a level they would never get from establishment politicians. We shouldn't assume these people don't want to delve deeply into the issues of the day, to have discussions that reflect the real nuances and complexity of political life. I don't buy into this idea that what you need is a simple soundbite everybody can instantly understand. That's a type of politics I don't feel that comfortable with. Part of the reason for running the campaign in this way was to show that we can do politics differently, that politics as usual is not essential. That is what motivates my involvement in this nascent party.

And the decision to set up the Camden People's Alliance in the aftermath of the election was presumably an attempt to show how this new type of politics can work in practice.

Exactly. Our MP, before he was prime minister and even before he was a prominent figure on the Labour front bench, was never an enthusiastic holder of regular local surgeries. Many people have felt very let down by him as a local representative. So, one of the things that the Camden People's Alliance has decided to do is to step in and fill that gap. We are holding 'community surgeries', where people who have particular needs, who are in crisis situations – and I didn't realise just how many people are in such predicaments until we started campaigning – can come to get support. We have groups with specialist expertise in housing, in the law, in healthcare, in education and so on. By getting them to share their knowledge we can enable the community to help the community, rather than relying on a distant and unpopular MP who has never been interested in local issues or local people.

My instinct is that when you establish these community power bases, it makes it more productive to engage in electoral politics, and it means that electoral representation can meet people's actual needs. In the CPA, our plan is to use community hustings to nominate candidates for local councils and for Parliament. If they are nominated, they will have to sign a pledge that not only commits them to the broad political principles I mentioned earlier but also to a process of local accountability, which includes very regular surgeries and engagement with their constituents on key decisions. This makes sure that they are constantly embedded in the communities they are serving.

I once attended an ANC caucus meeting in Parliament right after we'd all been elected as MPs, where Mandela walked into the room and said, 'So, who here thinks they're important now?' As he expected, a whole lot of people raised their hands. And then he made a simple and powerful point: the moment you think you're more important than the people who put you here – the people to whom you are accountable and who pay your salary every month – then you are no longer of value to those people, to this movement, to this Parliament or to this country. Those words informed how I saw my role as a member of Parliament, and they speak to the relationship I'd like to see between representatives of this new party and the people who elect them.

How do you view the relationship between organising within the community and within the party? Should we use the party to create a binding institutional link between this kind of local activity and national electoral campaigning?

In some localities, communities have already come together in a broad-based and effective way, while in other places that sort of organic organising isn't happening to the same degree. The party needs to respect these differences. There is no single model that will fit every part of the country. Where there are existing community initiatives, the party should work with them, but it should be up to the communities themselves to decide what relationship they want to have: whether they want to be subsumed into the party, affiliate to it or simply exist alongside it. In places where those initiatives are thinner on the ground, I think the party does have a responsibility to step in. Whereas in Camden you have political groups which have been active for years, and have an umbrella organisation to unite them, in somewhere like Clacton that sort of activity is more marginal and dispersed – so you might then need the party to create a structure for it.

If we take the CPA as an example, I think its members should be empowered to decide whether they want to remain a separate community organisation or to carry out their organising through the party structure, or to adopt a hybrid model in which it is linked to the party but not fully integrated. I suspect that in many cases a hybrid approach will be most desirable. There should be a similar flexibility and adaptability when it comes to running election campaigns. There are huge social and political differences between Camden and Southport and Blackburn, so the only way to win in all those places is to insist on local autonomy. It isn't necessary for candidates to have identical views, nor for the leadership to impose those views from the top down; that is the kind of authoritarian approach we're trying to get away from. There are certain people on the left who want a strong degree of centralised control: people who have long histories in formal politics, in electoral parliamentary politics. But neither Jeremy nor Zarah has that view, nor does the prospective membership of the party. I would very much like to see it established in a way that reflects a radically democratic ethos, with a launch conference that's as participatory as possible, so that it can continue in this vein once it begins to build real institutional power.

Different constituencies have their own distinct dynamics, which any national organising model risks neglecting if it's too rigid. But shouldn't we have a general sense of the demographics we're trying to reach, and the democratic structures that are most likely to activate them, so that we can create a

*coherent infrastructure for the party? Otherwise, we risk
dissolving the project into local particularism.*

There has to be a certain amount of targeting, but I don't
think it should be too narrow or restrictive. In Camden we
put most of our effort into council and social housing estates,
working-class neighbourhoods, marginalised communities,
and we saw a groundswell of support in those areas. But
when the results came in, we realised we had also done quite
well – better than we expected, and certainly better than the
Labour Party expected – in more affluent wards like Primrose
Hill. Why? Well, it was partly the Gaza phenomenon: people
who might be materially comfortable and still deeply *uncom-
fortable* with our government's participation in Israel's war.
But it also speaks to something much broader: a general
disaffection with politics, a sense that politicians are not
accountable, that democracy means nothing more than casting a vote every five years, and in the meantime we just have
to shut up and get on with our lives. This feeling transcends
traditional class categories.

So, that suggests to me that the left's typical approach,
of focusing on people who are economically disadvantaged
because of some aspect of their social identity, has limits
in contemporary Britain. There's a superb book by the
sociologist Dan Evans called *A Nation of Shopkeepers*,
which argues that since the Thatcher period the analytic
category of 'working class' has been unsettled by the rise
of the petty bourgeoisie – which includes both an older
contingent of small business owners and a newer cohort of
workers in industries like education, services and culture.
These are people who have done fairly well materially but
who are not being served by establishment politics. Their
lives are beset by constant uncertainty, and as a result

many of them are trending towards Reform (even though it is no less of an establishment party than Labour or the Conservatives).

In addition to this group, you have people who are actively involved in social movements, the vast majority of whom could broadly be defined as middle class. And then you have many people who aren't politically engaged at all, who feel they've been left behind, but who turned out in large numbers for many of the independent candidates who ran in 2024. Looking at this landscape, the question is how we bring together these different blocs: the historical working-class bases of the left, the petty bourgeois layers that are attracted to the far right, the middle-class activists who are mobilising against the status quo, and the abstentionists who have largely disengaged from party politics.

I think we can do it. But only if we demonstrate a real willingness to represent local people and follow through on their priorities with practical action, rather than adopting a position of political superiority where we assume to know what's best for them. The CPA hosted what was supposed to be a small community event a few months ago; we didn't advertise it very widely, and yet we had such an enormous turnout that about half the crowd couldn't fit in the room. Most of the people who came hadn't been involved in the 2024 campaign, but they had heard that there was an alternative type of politics developing in the area and they wanted to know more. When I chatted to them afterwards, they told me that the three issues they cared most about were Palestine, the cost of living and the state of our politicians. The last one is particularly salient in Camden, where one of our MPs is Starmer and the other is Tulip Siddiq, who is currently facing corruption charges in Bangladesh. But I've been going to meetings all over the country for the last few years and it's this same problem that keeps cropping up: our politicians embody a broken and self-serving mode of politics. If we stop to consider the true extent of that feeling, we can understand the need for this new party and its extraordinary potential.

Acknowledgements

Thanks to all the interviewees for taking part in the discussions. We invited Jeremy Corbyn to participate in this interview series, but it was not possible. Thanks also to Tariq Ali and everyone at Verso for their help.